Union and Communion
with CHRIST

Union and Communion
with CHRIST

by
Maurice Roberts

REFORMATION HERITAGE BOOKS
Grand Rapids, Michigan

Published by
Reformation Heritage Books
2965 Leonard St., NE
Grand Rapids, MI 49525
616-977-0599 / Fax 616-285-3246
e-mail: orders@heritagebooks.org
website: www.heritagebooks.org

Library of Congress Cataloging-in-Publication Data

Roberts, Maurice.
  Union and communion with Christ / by Maurice Roberts.
     p. cm.
  ISBN 978-1-60178-042-3 (pbk. : alk. paper)
  1. Spirituality. I. Title.
  BV4501.3.R633 2008
  248.4--dc22

                           2008013956

---

*For additional Reformed literature, both new and used, request a free
book list from Reformation Heritage Books at the above address.*

Table of Contents

Foreword

Union with Christ has always been one of the most important themes of the Christian life. This is particularly true in the Reformed faith. John Calvin's writings are so permeated with the theme of union with Christ that it becomes his focus for Christian faith and practice. Calvin writes, "That joining together of Head and members, that indwelling of Christ in our hearts — in short, that mystical union — are accorded by us the highest degree of importance, so that Christ, having been made ours, makes us sharers with him in the gifts with which he has been endowed" *(Institutes,* 3.11.9).

Union with Christ, which is one of the gospel's greatest mysteries, is possible by grace because Christ took on our human nature, filling it with His virtue. This union in turn produces through Spirit-worked faith communion with Christ, by which believers participate in Christ's benefits. Communion with Christ is the result of the Spirit's work, which is astonishing and experiential rather than comprehendible. The Holy Spirit is the link that binds the believer to Christ and the channel through which Christ is communicated. Through this union and communion with Christ, believers are empowered by the Spirit to live and grow in Christ so that they may increasingly walk with the triune God and come increasingly to know

Him as their heavenly Father, redeeming Savior, and sanctifying Spirit.

The grand acts of redemption—the sufferings, death, resurrection, and ascension of Christ; and the outpouring of His Spirit—are of little benefit if we are not so united with Jesus that we find our life and death in Him. In *Union and Communion with Christ,* Maurice Roberts offers eighteen warm, experiential meditations on the Christian's union with Christ and its accompanying fellowship. These reflections probe the essence of this blessed union, examine its evidences, and revel in its benefits.

Writing at a clearly understood level and aiming for spiritual edification, Roberts' book works well as a daily devotional. It will stimulate your mind, prick your conscience, and win your heart.

Roberts covers much in this little book without explaining away the mystery of union with Christ and without becoming overly polemic. Here is angels' food for the beginner in grace and the most advanced believer. Here also is sufficient material to move the unsaved, by the Spirit's work, to desire a true relationship with God. Here is Christianity experienced in the soul and spilling over into daily life. Take it and read it slowly, meditatively, and prayerfully and, by grace use it to appreciate and love your Savior more.

—Joel R. Beeke

The Love which Believers Owe to Christ

No beings owe greater gratitude and love to the Lord Jesus Christ than those who know Him as their Savior. The angels owe Him love and devotion as their Lord and God. This devotion they demonstrate by obediently carrying out Christ's wishes. They serve Him in a host of ways. They protect His people on earth (Dan. 3:28). They escort the souls of His people to glory at death (Luke 16:22). They minister to believers in this present life (Heb. 1:14). They gather out all the godless and the hypocrites at the end of the world and "cast them into a furnace of fire" (Matt. 13:42). They will, when the last trumpet sounds, "gather together all his elect from the four winds, from one end of heaven to the other" (Matt. 24:31).

But, great as the angels are in honor, they are not so close to Christ in this life as believers are. And they are not to be so close to Him in the eternal state of heaven as believers are to be. This is clear for several reasons. Christ "took not on him the nature

of angels; but he took on him the seed of Abraham"
(Heb. 2:16). Implied in this profound statement is the
truth that, when angels sinned and fell, there was no
Savior given to redeem them. They are "reserved in
everlasting chains under darkness unto the judgment
of the great day" (Jude 6). Fallen angels have no gospel, no hope, no Redeemer. But we fallen sinners
have Jesus offered to us. What a high privilege — and
how we should love Christ!

Then, too, as we see from the above statement in
Hebrews 2:16, Christ has come closer to us than to
the angels in that He has taken our nature and united
it to Himself: "The word was made flesh and dwelt
among us" (John 1:14). Christ is, uniquely among
all beings whatsoever, both God and man. Since His
incarnation, our Lord has had not only His eternal
divine nature but also a perfect human nature. Hence
Christ regards His believing people as His "brethren."
This is wonderfully expressed in the New Testament:
"In all things it behoved him to be made like unto his
brethren" (Heb. 2:17). Now, if the second Person of
the ever-blessed Godhead has taken to Himself our
nature, how much we should be grateful to Him! And
how much we should adore and love Him!

But we must go on to add more. Not only has the
blessed Lord Jesus taken our nature, He has lived
in it a perfect life. Only in this one instance do we
see a perfect human life. Jesus alone among all who
ever lived has lived a spotless and a sinless life. He
both dignified our nature by a life of total obedience

to His Father and gave to all believers the benefits of His own perfect life. For we say that this "active obedience" of Christ is imputed to us when we come to believe in Him. What a wealthy and rich gift this is!

To all the above we must add that this Jesus has still further placed us in His debt by dying for us the accursed death of the cross and by rising again in our nature from the dead. By so doing, He has still further enriched us in a variety of ways. One way is by "blotting out the handwriting of ordinances that was against us...nailing it to his cross" (Col. 2:14). That is to say, He has disannulled any and every aspect of God's law as far as that law might have power to condemn God's people.

Additionally, by death and resurrection, Christ has "spoiled principalities and powers" so as to make "a shew of them openly, triumphing over them in it" (Col. 2:15). In a word, our Lord has solved every problem, which we, as guilty sinners, once faced: the condemning power of God's law, the stranglehold that satanic powers had over mankind since the Fall, and the gloomy prospect of eternal death. For all this, our Savior Jesus Christ deserves our utmost gratitude and love.

But there is more still to be said. Christ, though now the conqueror of all His and our enemies, is actively engaged in a ceaseless work of intercession on our behalf, daily ensuring, as He watches over us, that not one of those for whom He suffered and died will be lost (John 17:15). Our perseverance to the end depends on His unfailing faithfulness to us in the comforting promise, "I am with you alway, even to the end of the world" (Matt. 28:20).

The crowning mercy will be when Christ raises us from the dead and, as Judge, pronounces us to be fully justified in His righteousness and eligible to enter into the glory of heaven. In this exalted state, we shall know Christ's love towards us as no other created beings will do. For we, being His church, shall be to Him "as a bride adorned for her husband" (Rev. 21:2). We shall at last enter into the palace of heavenly glory with Him and experience eternal "gladness and rejoicing" (Ps. 45:15).

Everything that Christ ever did, He did for our sakes who believe in Him. And our proper reaction must be to desire to show our attachment and our gratitude to Christ in consciously seeking to love and worship Him. The nearer we see our relationship to be to anyone, the stronger we feel our affection to be. We feel strange with strangers, but we are closer to cousins — closer still to brothers and sisters, and closest of all to husband or wife. This is the most tender, sweet, and intimate of all relationships.

Since this is so, our Lord and Savior has written to us in His Word that we are regarded by Him as in this supremely close and tender relationship: "We are members of his body, of his flesh, and of his bones" (Eph. 5:30). The church, then, is the "new Eve" who is given to the Second Adam to be His "helpmeet" in the relationship of mutual delight and affection in that period of history which will begin after time itself has ceased to exist.

The relationship, then, in which Christian believers stand with Jesus Christ, is the closest of all relationships, both in this life and in the life to come. Believers have union and communion with Christ—both in grace and in glory.

This deep and wondrous truth is written very clearly into the warp and woof of Holy Scripture. Believers, first, were chosen by God the Father "in him before the foundation of the world" (Eph. 1:4). By God's gracious, sovereign, and undeserved election, we were "given" to Christ in eternity past (John 17:2, 6). In the course of time, the elect in Christ are brought to Christ by a secret inner impulse of God's power, through which they "come" to Christ as Savior (John 6:37, 44). When they believe savingly in Christ, they become spiritually united to Him and are described as being "in Christ." This phrase is used frequently in the New Testament Scriptures to denote the close and unbreakable bond of union and fellowship, which all believers have with the Lord Jesus.

The phrase "in Christ," then, must not be confined only to our "*believing* in Christ," in which the emphasis is upon our placing our trust in Christ as the object of our faith. Precious as this aspect of our relationship to Christ is, it is not the whole of our relationship to God's dear Son. The true believer is "in Christ" as Christ is the head of a covenant. As all those *not* in Christ are declared to be federally "in

Adam" (1 Cor. 15:22), so all those who *are* "in Christ" are federally related to Him. The consequences of federal relationship are immense, and they are eternal.

The inescapable consequences of being "in Adam" as a covenant head are these: the imputation to us of his first sin, the condemnation which sin merits, and death, in the sense of eternal punishment. Conversely, the happy consequences of being "in Christ" as a covenant head are the imputation to us of Christ's righteousness, the justification merited by Christ's obedience, and eternal life. Therefore, the federal implications of being "in Christ" have the most serious bearing on our life in this world and that which is to come (see Rom. 5:12 – 19).

It is a heart-warming truth to realize our intimate relationship as Christians to the Lord Jesus Christ. He is "THE LORD OUR RIGHTEOUSNESS" (Jer. 23:6). He is "made unto us wisdom, and righteousness, and sanctification, and redemption" (1 Cor. 1:30). Christ is "our peace" (Eph. 2:14). Our "life is hid with Christ in God" (Col. 3:3). We are "crucified" with Him (Gal. 2:20), and we have been "buried with him by baptism into death" (Rom. 6:4). As Christ has been resurrected so we, being in Him, will be raised to life at the Last Day, for "as in Adam all die, even so in Christ shall all be made alive" (1 Cor. 15:22). The reference here clearly is to the bodily resurrection of all true believers. During our life in this world, being children of Adam, "we have borne the image of the earthly." But when our Lord returns we shall at once and forever after "bear the image of the heavenly" (1 Cor. 15:49). Our resurrection body will be perfectly suited to our everlasting life with Christ in the kingdom of glory.

In the light of our understanding of the close relationship which we have as believers who are "in Christ," we cannot and must not do less than marvel at God's goodness to us. Our duty in our earthly life is to seek to increase in a humble and sincere love for that blessed Savior, Jesus Christ, to whom we owe so much.

2

The Union of Believers with Christ

The union that believers have with Christ in this life is perhaps nowhere more clear than in Christ's reference to the vine and its branches: "I am the true vine, and my Father is the husbandman. Every branch in me that beareth not fruit he taketh away: and every branch that beareth fruit he purgeth it, that it may bring forth more fruit" (John 15:1–2). How are we to interpret this passage of Scripture?

All of our spiritual life, if we have any, must come from the Lord Jesus Christ. It flows from Him to us, as believers, by the gracious activity of His Holy Spirit. The evidence of our having this relationship of union with Christ is the fruit which is seen in our lives. This fruit is not measured in worldly terms, like success in business or commerce, but is to be recognized by the measure of our conformity to the character of Christ Himself: "Love, joy, peace, longsuffering, gentleness, goodness, faith, meekness, temperance" (Gal. 5:22–23). To have a character and life which reflect these fruits is a sure evidence that we are "in Christ" and are being inwardly transformed into His likeness "from glory to glory" (2 Cor. 3:18).

When, in the passage given above (John 15:1–2), Christ speaks of a "branch in me that beareth not fruit," He speaks of the person who professes to be a Christian but who has never truly come into a spiritual union with Christ. Great attention should be paid to this warning. Scripture and experience alike teach us that not all who profess to be Christians are truly "in Him." "Many will say to me in that day [i.e. the Day of Judgment], Lord, Lord, have we not prophesied in thy name? and in thy name have cast out devils? and in thy name done many wonderful works? And then will I profess unto them, I never knew you: depart from me, ye that work iniquity" (Matt. 7:22–23). In these and similar words, Christ warns all who profess to be His to look for evidence of their conversion elsewhere than in their outward works. Hypocrites and false Christians may do the things that are here made the basis of their hopes. Judas Iscariot did so; many who are now in hell were once preachers or theological lecturers.

The only evidence of real Christian faith and life is to be seen in the *character* we possess. Where Christ is in a man's soul, the fruits of love, peace, and holiness will be visible. The Holy Spirit is not so much given to impart gifts to men as to create in them a likeness to Christ. Grace is above gifts; gifts can be counterfeited by Satan, but true love, faith, and holiness cannot be.

The true beginning of a person's union with Christ is not at his baptism or at his entrance into church membership. The real spiritual life begins when we are brought into living and vital union with Jesus Christ. This occurs the instant we are "born again" of "water and of the Spirit" (John 3:5). The reference here to "water" is figurative, like the reference to the "vine" in John 15. Christ means that the new birth is an act of God in the soul which cleanses it from defilement and begins for it a life of fellowship with God. The "natural man" is a man who is "sensual, having not the Spirit" (Jude 19). He is carnal, united to the broken law of God, which can tell him what to do but cannot impart energy to him to keep it. At our new birth, however, God gives us power to keep the commandments—not perfectly, but sincerely. The man who is born again is in a new relationship with Christ and his soul is now the subject of a lifelong influence of Christ's Holy Spirit by which he more and more shuns the things that displease God.

On the other hand, the merely nominal Christian, however pious his words, secretly loves the things of the world. He does not have a renewed nature. He has no influences of saving grace. At best, he has some measure of common grace to restrain him; but his heart is secretly in the world and his thoughts are of the world. Christ says ominously that the unfruitful branches will be removed, sooner or later, by the hand of God and be cast into the "fire" and "burned" (John 15:2, 6). The false Christian may not appear to be false for some considerable time. He may appear to be sound in the faith and upright in his life. He may become a worker for God and gain a name for himself. Nevertheless, because he is not in vital spiritual union with Jesus Christ, he can only come to a sad end. Sooner or later, he will wither and die. And, most fearfully, he must be cast into the "fire" of which Christ elsewhere says it shall "not be quenched" (Mark 9:46).

This deeply serious teaching from the lips of the Son of God shows us that the subject of our union with Christ is not of secondary importance, but is the most vital of subjects. If all who make profession of being Christian would pay more attention to this part of our Lord's teaching, they might benefit their souls and better their eternal destiny. Neither "prophecy," nor "tongues speaking," nor public speaking, nor "miracles of healing" are nearly as important as having union between our souls and Jesus Christ.

Here surely we are to find the source of all the declension and backsliding in the history of the church of Christ. The history of most churches shows the same trend: the first generation is godly; the second is learned; the third is worldly. The root problem is that, as time goes on, the attachment to Christ and His gospel becomes less and less. The first generation of a church loves Christ and truth with fervor and with passion. The next generation loves with a more intellectual but a less ardently devotional love. They know the truth more as a thing of the mind than of the heart. Hence, in the next generation, the gospel is received in a more or less formal way. This generation wants a foot in the church and a foot in the world. They do not live to be "different" from the world. They like the world's ways and they aim to enjoy them as far as they can. The result is that, being lukewarm, Christ says, "I will spew thee out of my mouth" (Rev. 3:16).

If we intend to get safely to heaven, the greatest need we have is to make sure we are engrafted into Christ. To have His Spirit truly in our souls is to be in the one and only place of safety. It is to be "in Christ" and "in God the Father" (1 Thess. 1:1), because he who has the Son has also the Father (2 John 9). Here alone and here emphatically is safety and security; "neither shall any man pluck them out of my hand" (John 10:28) nor "out of my Father's hand" (John 10:29).

The point to which our Lord brings us by His solemn teaching is one of self-examination: "Let a man examine himself," says the Word of God (1 Cor. 11:28). It is not sufficient to have made a profession of faith in Christ as Savior. We must also take an honest look into our own heart and life. If we are truly Christ's people, we must show it by a life of holiness and godliness. It is for this reason that Paul closes his epistle to the Corinthians with this challenging exhortation: "Examine yourselves, whether ye be in the faith; prove your own selves. Know ye not that Jesus Christ is in you, except ye be reprobates?" (2 Cor. 13:5).

Self-examination is necessary in case a man should conclude hastily that he is "in Christ" when this is not so. Many build before they have "digged deep" (Luke 6:48). Many "receive the word" at first but are not really "rooted" in the salvation of Jesus Christ (Matt. 13:6). The great need is that we make sure of the *main* thing: "Am I truly united to Christ in a living union or am I but a dead and fruitless branch?"

It would be a blessing to multitudes who hurry along the various paths of Christian witness and Christian service if they were to pause amidst their busy schedules and make sure that they have the one thing needful (Luke 10:42). How tragic must be the case of all those who throw themselves into church life and church work under the impression that they are on the way to glory and are not! How awful must be the state of mind of those who, having rushed through life in the busy routines of a professing Christian, find themselves at last in a lost eternity! This discovery comes too late for repentance or amendment. Once the pit of darkness closes its mouth over any man, it must keep him there — in total darkness. How terrible must be the pangs of conscience of all who preached to others what they did not have in their own hearts! How complete must be the despair of those whose hope of heaven was ill founded! Looking for a place in heaven all their lives, they now find themselves in hell with the wicked of all ages.

That such self-deception is all too possible is clearly shown by Christ: "The children of the kingdom shall be cast out into outer darkness: there shall be weeping and gnashing of teeth" (Matt. 8:12). There is only one way to ensure we do not suffer so terrible a disappointment. It is to "abide in Christ" as those who are truly in a vital union with Him.

3

The Nature of Our Union with Christ

As we have seen, there are several illustrations used in Scripture to show the different aspects of our union as believers with Christ: the vine and its branches, a building on its foundation, the husband and wife within the relationship of marriage, etc. No one illustration can convey all aspects of our spiritual relationship with the blessed Son of God. There is always more, and there is always mystery. It is, truly, a "mystical union." It is many-sided and its depths and heights are far beyond our comprehension in this life.

There is, even at first sight, a wonderful variety in the scriptural language referring to this subject. We are, as believers, said to be "in Christ" (Eph. 1:3). Then Christ is said to be "in you" (Col. 1:27). Christ is also said to "dwell in your hearts" (Eph. 3:17). We are to have His "mind" in us (Phil. 2:5). We are those who have "learned" from Him, have "been taught" by Him (Eph. 4:21), have heard his voice (John 10:27), "walk" in Him (Col 2:6), and are to be conformed to "his image" (Col. 3:10). We are "of his flesh and of his bones" (Eph. 5:30), have been "given" to Him by God the Father from eternity past (John 17:6), are His "brethren" (Heb. 2:11–12), and share a common "life" with Him (Col. 3:4). He makes continual intercession for us until we come to glory (Heb. 7:25). He now reigns until all His and our enemies are at last "put under him" (Heb. 2:8). So great is His love for us that Christ will keep the whole world in being and delay His glorious return until the very last of His blood-bought children are brought "to repentance" (2 Peter 3:9).

It is clear from the above scriptural references that our mystical relationship with Christ is many-sided and consists of a great number of interconnected strands. Since this is so, it is of great profit and importance for us to attempt to draw out at least some of the elements which go to make up the intensely complex relationship we have with the Son of God. The fact that there are depths entirely beyond us does not absolve us from the duty of seeking to explore the various strands of this great doctrine.

1. First, we must point to *the plan of God in eternity past*. This is the proper place to begin. It is entirely owing to God's eternal purpose before the world began that we should have any relationship of this kind with the great Son of God. The term "election" has sometimes been thought to frighten off believers, or else becomes a subject of controversy; but it ought

not to be so. "Election" is a term of love — indeed, the highest form of love conceivable.

Election means that action of God before mankind existed by which the great Lord of heaven and earth chose to give to unworthy creatures all the richest favor and blessings we are capable of receiving: solid happiness to all eternity.

This happiness, God determined, would not be earthly perfection in a paradise of pleasures here below, but an enjoyment of fellowship with God in Christ for all eternity. In this way, God purposed to raise us up to the highest honor and privilege of which any creature is capable: the eternal enjoyment of God Himself in all the fullness in which He exists.

This happiness would be both inward, in the subjective enjoyment of God's Spirit conveying to the souls of believers the felt ecstasy of God's love for them in Christ, and the outward happiness of seeing God in the beatific vision. This is the vision of God in all His uncreated and ineffable beauty and glory, by which the elect believers would be ravished in their souls as they enjoy God forever.

We must not look beyond God's own secret will for any explanation of His eternal election. God is not answerable to any being for His actions or decisions. It is sufficient for us as creatures to know that we, if we are believers in union with Christ, do not believe because we willed ourselves to do so, but because God set His love on us from eternity past. This act of God, and not our willpower, determined the change in our lives by which we became God's children and are now united to Christ.

2. A second aspect of our relationship to Christ that calls for mention is *transformation of character and behavior*. The merely outward "Christian" may be able to answer questions correctly with his lips, but he has no real transformation of heart and character. Various scriptural expressions bear witness to the reality of this inward change in those who are Christ's. They are "not of the world" (John 17:16). They are "salt" and "light" (Matt. 5:13–14). They are "temples" of the Holy Spirit (1 Cor. 6:19). They are "strangers and pilgrims" (1 Pet. 2:11) in this world. Their real citizenship is in heaven (Phil. 3:20). Of no other people can these and similar things be said but of the elect who have come to experience the reality of life in Christ. In their character, they are different from all other people.

The inward consciousness of being different from the rest of mankind might make the elect proud except for the realization that they have of fundamental Bible truths. For one thing, they are humbled at the recollection of their sinfulness before Christ brought them into union with Himself and made them holy. Also, they are keenly aware that they fall far short of their privileges, and they rather grieve at how like the world they still are than boast because of their own holiness.

This difference of outlook is how the true child of

God is distinguished from the hypocrite. The hypocrite, who is not truly united to Christ, secretly loves the world and glories in his religious achievement. But the man who is genuinely united to Christ grieves to be so unlike his Master and to be, at his very best, an unprofitable servant (Luke 17:10).

God, in His wisdom, has made lowliness a sure mark of true union with Christ and pride a certain sign of the absence of any genuine union with Christ. The true believer is an heir of glory and has all good things in prospect. But he mourns and is not at ease with himself in this life. His standard is perfection and he cannot be content with the small measure of his attainment in holiness. On the other hand, those who are not in Christ, but merely profess to be, are confident and self-assured because they have never seen with the eye of the soul that absolute purity which God requires and which only Christ has exemplified on earth.

3. A further aspect of the union the believer has with Christ is his sense of being always *ill at ease in this world*. He is aware of being not at home here below. The worldly man is at home in the world and he is comfortable with it as it now is, but the believer shares with Christ a deep instinct that the world is enemy ground and hostile territory.

It is clear that Jesus Christ was not in His element at any point in this world. From the cradle to the grave, our Lord was pursued and persecuted in this life. The most religious as well as the most unreligious were His enemies and resented all that He was and did. Only the small company of men and women in the circle of our Lord's friends truly loved Him or truly shared His attitude toward this world. So it must always be.

To be in union with Christ is to have fellowship with Him here below as a "man of sorrows and acquainted with grief" (Isa. 53:3). Few things about the life of Christ are more remarkable than that "the world was made by him, and the world knew him not" (John 1:10). The graceless world is enemy territory for all who love Christ. One of the inevitable shadows in the life of a true believer is that he must live here patiently in this present world, knowing that the world around him hates all that he is and all that he stands for.

4. A final aspect of a believer's union with Christ is *his hope*. By this, we mean his forward-looking expectation of ultimate happiness and relaxation in the world to come. Here he must "watch and pray." Here he is called on, as was Christ, to be a stranger in a strange land. But, in the world to come, he knows he will have all that his heart could desire: heaven, glory, and God forever.

To the formal Christian this is ridiculous. The formal Christian wants at least some of his good things here and now. The formalist wears a mask of religion but his eyes are very much on the good things of this present world. Not so the man who is "in Christ." He shudders at the way men of the world live for what cannot satisfy the soul. The life of worldly men seems to the godly like the first chapter of hell itself: no enjoyment of God, no holiness, no inward peace.

Dear reader, do not rest in a mere acquaintance with the things of God. Be satisfied in no aspect of religion until you are assured that you are truly in union with the Lord Jesus Christ.

4

A Union More
Enduring than Time

The union which believers have with Christ is stronger than all others. The bond of friendship, unless it be friendship "in the Lord," will be severed at death, if not before. Our precious family ties with parents, siblings, and other relatives, if not "in Christ," must be dissolved in the grave. Alas, the pagan nations of old were all too right when, at death, they bade one another an *eternal* farewell. It is so still. The ties that bind us together, if not eternally cemented by a saving relationship to Jesus Christ, will all soon be broken forever. Only the bond of divine grace will last. Only as we leave one another "in the Lord" do we have an unbreakable tie and an undying hope of being united happily again.

The one bond, then, which time and circumstance cannot break, is that which we have with our blessed Redeemer, Jesus Christ. Death has now no power over Him; and once the Last Day comes, death will have no more power over His believing people. Not for nothing has Christ entered the cold grave for His people. He is "the death of death" and "the firstborn from the dead" (Col. 1:18). Christ has become "the firstfruits of them that slept" (1 Cor. 15:20). To His people He is able to say, "Because I live ye shall live also" (John 14:19).

The implication of these and all the similar promises of God to believers is that the union which we now enjoy with the Lord Jesus Christ will never be ruptured. Neither Satan, sin, death nor any other force or agency of darkness will ever disunite what God has united. Through God's unspeakable grace and love, we who are now in life united to Christ shall be united with Him forever. This has been the comfort and the hope of God's saints in all ages. With this conviction in his soul, Job cried out, "I know that my Redeemer liveth" (Job 19:25). Fortified by this assurance, David, on his deathbed, exclaimed, "He [God] hath made with me an everlasting covenant, ordered in all things and sure" (2 Sam. 23:5). And, a millennium later, Paul the apostle, with his day of death clearly before him, declared, "Henceforth there is laid up for me a crown of righteousness" (2 Tim. 4:8). O mercy beyond all other mercies! God's believing people will never be separated "from the love of God which is in Christ Jesus our Lord" (Rom. 8:39)!

The reason why this bond to Christ is the only one that will endure beyond death is that Christ has fully and perfectly satisfied all the demands of God's justice and thereby removed the sentence of eternal punishment from His children. Our guarantee of eternal fellowship with the Triune God is the empty grave. The righteous God has received such a rich ransom for His people that His justice is infinitely satisfied.

The divine anger and wrath at our sin is quenched absolutely and everlastingly. Christ has given us a robe of perfect righteousness so that the righteousness God requires is fully and entirely met. There is in the shed blood of Jesus a "how much more!" The Scriptures draw attention to this abundant adequacy of Christ's finished work: "How much more shall the blood of Christ, who through the eternal Spirit offered himself without spot to God, purge your conscience from dead works to serve the living God?" (Heb. 9:14).

All this is not to deny that there are powerful forces within and outside us that threaten and menace the security of our union with Christ. The world, the flesh, and the devil all exert their influence against our assured hope of eternal security. They besiege our souls and strive to break, if only they could, our bond of union with Christ. Dark forces of temptation whisper loudly in our ear at some times of our lives that we have "sinned away our hope of pardon," or else "grieved away God's Spirit forever." How the powers of hell would love, if only they might, to snap the tie that binds us to a Savior's love and protection! These powers of hell are fearfully real and fearfully strong. In the case of all who are false believers they will be successful.

To warn us of the danger of being religious but not truly converted, God has shown us the "last words" of religious men who had no saving union with Jesus Christ. Hear Saul's sad admission: "I have played the fool and have erred exceedingly" (1 Sam. 26:21). More tragic still, listen to the "last words" of Judas Iscariot: "I have sinned in that I have betrayed the innocent blood" (Matt. 27:4).

No less dreadful, let us hear the warnings in the book of Hebrews, as that writer portrays the crime of some of this world's Christ-rejecters: "They crucify to themselves the Son of God afresh, and put him to an open shame" (Heb. 6:6). They have, says God again, "trodden underfoot the Son of God, and have counted the blood of the covenant...an unholy thing" (Heb. 10:29). Such intense guilt can scarcely be grasped by our finite minds. But, clearly, some people are guilty of it—and will have to answer for it.

Be the powers of sin and hell never so strong, however, those who humbly trust in a crucified and glorified Savior will prove to be "more than conquerors" at last. The "meek...shall inherit the earth" (Matt. 5:5), and the "wayfaring men, though fools, shall not err" in their patient pilgrimage to the heavenly city of God. The bond of union which holds us to Christ is a silken thread more durable than bonds of adamantine steel.

The bond of union between Christ and His people will endure all through life—it will endure beyond death. It will continue after the resurrection and beyond the Judgment Day. It will remain intact in the "new heavens and new earth" where God's people are to live forever at last. Hence, Christ can say such comforting words as these: "I am the resurrection, and the life: he that believeth in me, though he were dead, yet shall he live: and whosoever liveth and believeth in me shall never die" (John 11:25–26). Could we ever want a greater assurance or comfort than this?

At death, the soul leaves the body until the Judgment Day. It enters into a place suited to its own moral and spiritual condition. This is what we refer to as the "intermediate state." It comprises a place of punishment for those who are not in Christ and a place of blessed rest for all who die in the Lord. Here the souls of God's people are instantly made perfect in holiness at the moment of death and they are happy and grateful to be at last with Christ. For this reason, the Apostle Paul regards death as preferable to life for the true believer: "To depart, and to be with Christ...is far better" (Phil. 1:23).

The Christian's soul in the intermediate state of glory is now perfectly holy and perfectly happy. But it is not complete. The body is an integral part of our human constitution. Christ has redeemed it and, therefore, it must share at last in the glorious heavenly state to come. It is still united to Him, even in the state of death. Though the body turns to dust, all the atoms of it are precious to the Lord Christ who died for it. He died for us in every aspect of our being, body and soul; hence, every part of the believer must benefit from His finished work. The body must rise in glory. It must be reunited with the soul and partake of the great redemption which Jesus has accomplished.

Marvelous as the redemption of the soul is, we must not overlook the importance that the Bible places on the resurrection of the body also. Here is "mystery" indeed (1 Cor. 15:51)! The body must benefit also from the union we have with the Son of God: "This corruptible must put on incorruption, and this mortal must put on immortality" (1 Cor. 15:53).

Every disfigurement that sin and death place upon our body in this life must be removed in the Great Day. The entire church of God will then be without "spot, or wrinkle, or any such thing" (Eph. 5:27). Christ is able to "subdue all things unto himself" and, as He rejuvenates the entire universe, He will "change our vile body, that it might be fashioned like unto his glorious body" (Phil. 3:21).

Because the union we have with Christ is indissoluble, none who are truly His will be lost; they all will come home to glory and to God. It will ensure the safety and well-being of our soul and it will bring our body forth from the grave. In that hour we, as believers, will "shine forth as the sun in the kingdom" of our Father (Matt. 13:43). Christ, as Judge, will acquit and admit all His people to the heavenly kingdom and to the wedding feast of the Lamb.

Could any topic be more comforting or more

delightful to God's people in this weary, sin-sick world? All sorrows will be over in that blessed place above. All sins will be pardoned. All service done for Christ will be abundantly rewarded. All our weaknesses and blemishes will be removed. It is clear from what the Scriptures tell us about the benefits of union with Christ that they far exceed any other benefits the mind of man has ever conceived. No wonder God has told us, "Eye hath not seen, nor ear heard, neither have entered into the heart of man, the things which God hath prepared for them that love him" (1 Cor. 2:9)! All the clever ideas of clever men are as dross compared with the glory that God has so graciously devised, planned, and prepared for all who believe in Jesus, our holy and blessed Savior!

Dear reader, is your soul united with this Savior in an eternal bond of union? If not, seek Him with all your heart until you find Him. You will find Him when you seek Him with all your heart.

5

Abiding in Christ

The believer's relationship with Christ is a blessing of God's gracious act of regeneration: "Of him [God the Father] are ye in Christ Jesus" (1 Cor. 1:30). We do not possess the ability to place ourselves into the relationship of union with the Son of God; neither do we cooperate with God to engraft ourselves into Christ. This action is monergistic — that is to say, it is entirely of God.

This must be so because our new birth is a work of omnipotence which does not merely *adjust* us to spiritual things but *recreates* us, so that we are said to be "a new creation" (2 Cor. 5:17). Similarly, we are described as God's "workmanship, *created* in Christ Jesus" (Eph. 2:10).

That the act of regeneration is wholly of God without our cooperation is made clearer still by Paul's allusion to the creation of the natural world: "For God, who commanded the light to shine out of darkness, hath shined in our hearts, to give the light of the knowledge of the glory of God in the face of

Jesus Christ" (2 Cor. 4:6). We no more cooperate in our new birth than we did in the original creation of the universe in which we live. Creation is entirely and exclusively God's own work. To suppose that we cooperate in it is to assume powers that we do not possess. It is also to take away from the debt of gratitude and praise which, as believers, we owe to God alone.

However, once we are united to Christ in our newly created state, we are laid under the lifelong duty and obligation to "abide in Christ." Our Lord puts it in more than one form: "Abide in me" (John 15:4). A little later He says, "Continue ye in my love" (John 15:9). It is clear that there is duty and obligation set before us in the context of our union and communion with the Lord Jesus Christ. We as believers have a duty and an obligation to keep up and to preserve the relationship with Christ which the new birth, without cooperation on our part, has so graciously bestowed upon us.

This should not surprise us. The relationship with the Lord Jesus we as believers are brought into is not a mechanical one but is a spiritual one. That is to say, it involves us in maintaining and promoting the bond of love that exists between our blessed Redeemer and us. Every relationship is a two-sided thing. As in marriage and in all our other earthly relationships, so in our union with the Son of God, we are laid under obligation to behave in such a way that the harmony and stability of the relationship is advanced and not retarded.

There are ways of misinterpreting the Lord's command to "abide" in Him which are misleading and harmful. Our Lord does not mean by "abiding" in Him that we should attempt to be entirely passive, as has sometimes been supposed. For example, it was once the slogan of a well-known conference in the United Kingdom to say to Christians that they should "Let go and let God." This slogan was used to discourage all thought of striving, fighting, or contending in the mature Christian life. The real road to advanced Christian maturity was said to be to relax and to be as passive in the union we have with Christ as the branch is in the vine. After all, it was said, a branch receives its sap automatically and without effort—and so produces its fruit.

There is more than one objection to this way of interpreting Christ's command to us to "abide" in Him. One objection is that it presses Christ's illustration of the vine too far. Christ's use of the vine and its fruit is clearly intended to explain our relationship of dependence upon Him for grace and blessing. We must not strain the analogy by urging more than this point.

Another objection to the slogan "Let go and let God" is that it runs counter to what Christ goes on to inform us as to our duty as we abide in Him: "If ye keep my commandments, ye shall abide in my love; even as I have kept my Father's commandments and abide in his love" (John 15:10). It is not possible to interpret these words as if our one and only duty

as believers is to remain wholly passive in our relationship to Christ. The obligation given here is that
we are to keep His commandments—and the analogy for our obedience is to be nothing less than the
example of Christ's obedience. This analogy does not
lead us to think of pure passivity but rather of the
most strenuous activity to do God's will and to do it
in full, both in life and death.

For these reasons, it would be a mistake to allow
ourselves to suppose that our entire obligation within
the bond of union with Christ is satisfied if we "let
go." On the contrary, says our Lord, "keep my commandments" (v. 10). So we need to turn our attention
to see what is involved in this duty.

It is obvious from the context that our Lord means
by "his commandments" that we are to pay the utmost
attention to the duty of love to one another. There
are several references in the context to the importance of Christian love, especially in the words: "This
is my commandment, That ye love one another, as
I have loved you" (v. 12). Is there here, then, a plain
reference to the Ten Commandments? Most certainly
there is. The Ten Commandments are the perpetual
and unchanging rule of life, of which Christ elsewhere
says, "Think not that I am come to destroy the law, or
the prophets: I am not come to destroy, but to fulfill"
(Matt. 5:17). The Ten Commandments will never cease
to be our rule of duty so long as we are in this world.
We are, as Christians, not saved by keeping them; we
are saved in order that we might keep them.

It is not the case, as has sometimes been supposed, that God's moral law is now replaced by a new law of love, which differs from the Ten Commandments. The way to love is by a careful keeping of the Ten Commandments. Paul puts it in these words: "Love worketh no ill to his neighbour: therefore love is the fulfilling of the law" (Rom. 13:10). There is only one adjustment to the moral law in New Testament times. Whereas before the resurrection of Christ the weekly Sabbath was on the last day of the week, now in New Testament times the weekly Sabbath is on the *first* day. This day is now obligatory on our consciences as the one day in seven on which we are to refrain from all unnecessary secular work and spend the day in the public and private exercises of God's worship.

In John 15, the Lord Jesus Christ does not call His people to a life of pure passivity but to a life of careful obedience to every duty implicit in the Ten Commandments. This is why the great Reformers, Luther and Calvin, and later the great Puritans, wrote extensively on the obligations laid upon us by each one of the Ten Commandments.

More importantly still, the apostles of Christ explain repeatedly that the Christian's practical and lifelong calling is to keep God's commandments. "Circumcision is nothing, and uncircumcision is nothing, but the keeping of the commandments of God" (1 Cor. 7:19). James refers to the moral law as "the royal law" (James 2:8) and he explains that to transgress God's law is to "commit sin" (James 2:9).

He implies that our duty is to "keep the whole law" (James 2:10). John is equally concerned to show that the Ten Commandments are our perpetual rule of life as believers. "He that saith, I know him [God], and keepeth not his commandments, is a liar, and the truth is not in him" (1 John 2:4).

In a word, Christ's words in John 15, in which He urges us to keep His commandments, are His explanation as to how we are to maintain our communion with Him: it is by a conscientious obedience to the will of God as that is summarized in the Ten Commandments. The essence of this obedience is to love God with all our heart and our neighbor as ourselves. As John tells us, this is an "old commandment," which we had centuries before Christ's incarnation. But it is also new because, with the coming of Christ, grace is given through the gospel to believers worldwide, and the effect of grace in the soul is love, especially love to fellow-believers (1 John 2:7 – 8).

Our union with Christ, if we are truly "in him," cannot be broken. But our communion with Christ will be dimmed and weakened if we do not carefully attend to the duty of a full-souled and full-hearted obedience to the revealed will of God in Scripture.

A man who professes Christ as Savior but has no love for his fellow-believers and no conscientious concern to keep the Ten Commandments is not a Christian. He has no light of grace in his soul and is self-deceived. "He that hateth his brother is in darkness, and walketh in darkness, and knoweth not whither he goeth, because that darkness hath blinded his eyes" (1 John 2:11).

Hence, if we mean to enjoy in its fullness the love and joy of soul that Christ affords to those who are in union with Him, we must attend carefully to the duties which His Word enjoins upon us day by day. This is not a passive but an active posture of soul. Reader, are you endeavoring in every way to work out your salvation to God's glory? If so, you will enjoy an inward feast of Christ's love.

6

Christ, Our Life and Our Righteousness

The elect people of God are "given" to Christ from eternity past (John 17:2, 6) but they do not come into vital union with Him until their effectual calling and regeneration. They have no spiritual life in them, neither are they justified, until this union with Christ takes place in the course of their lives here in this world. Before the elect come to Christ as Savior and Lord, they are "dead in trespasses and sins" (Eph. 2:1) and "children of wrath, even as others" (Eph. 2:3). The decree of God's eternal election ensures that the elect all come to Christ and become united spiritually with Him. But these benefits of salvation, life, righteousness, and peace with God do not enter into our experience until we become one with the Lord Jesus Christ.

We must distinguish properly between the decree of election and what it accomplishes. It is true that God sets His love on His elect from before the foundation of the world (Eph. 1:4). It is true to say that God has predestinated the elect to the privilege of becoming God's adopted children (Eph. 1:5). So the elect are loved from eternity past by God, and they are given to Christ to be redeemed and brought to glory.

But the elect do not enjoy the benefits of having spiritual life and enlightenment until they actually come to believe in Christ in the course of their life in this world. Only when the elect come to Christ and become united to Him do they have life, light, pardon, and peace. The instant they believe in Jesus, they have all these blessings at once.

The method by which God brings His elect to Himself is by "calling" them through the gospel. God ensures that each elect person by one means or another hears the gospel's message. This is referred to as the "outward call." It is the promise given to men everywhere that, upon faith in Christ and repentance, they will be saved. Both elect and non-elect hear this "outward call"; but, in the case of the elect, God puts forth a special divine influence that accompanies the gospel message. The result is that the elect are moved, affected, and awakened to a degree that others are not. This special influence of grace that God puts forth in the case of His elect is termed His "effectual calling." It ensures that the elect believe the gospel.

The gospel is to be preached to all men. God offers the promise of pardon and eternal life to all mankind, and the offer is freely and sincerely given. "Whosoever will" may come (Rev. 22:17). None are excluded except those who refuse the offer and reject the promise it delivers to lost mankind.

We do not know who the elect are and we have no right to restrict the gospel to any one group. We are to press the gospel's claims and its blessings on all men as far as we have opportunity. But, when all our preaching is done, the only ones who will believe unto salvation will be God's elect. Christ makes this clear with the words: "No man can come to me, except the Father which hath sent me draw him" (John 6:44).

The reason why the call of God the Father operates effectually in the elect is that God gives them the new birth along with the outward hearing of the gospel message. To them, therefore, the gospel comes "in power, and in the Holy Ghost, and in much assurance" (1 Thess. 1:5). So persuasive is the gospel's message to the elect that they embrace Christ for salvation and are inwardly moved to look to Christ's blood as the only way of having peace with God. Others may hear the same sermon and, for a time, be impressed by the gospel. But they never come to saving faith because their soul is not illuminated or empowered as the souls of the elect are.

The moment the soul of any person receives the new birth, he or she becomes spiritually united to Christ, our life and our righteousness. As an immediate consequence, therefore, of being now spiritually alive in Christ, the newly converted sinner believes in Christ. We cannot believe savingly in Christ until we are born again of God's Spirit. But, as soon as we are born again, we *do* believe. Indeed, we cannot but believe. This faith is said in Scripture, therefore, to be "the gift of God" (Eph. 2:8). It is the gift of God as a result of the new birth. We are spiritually transformed and, once we are united by faith to Christ, are said to be God's "workmanship, created in Christ Jesus unto good works" (Eph. 2:10). So, the faith by which we believe savingly in Jesus Christ is described as "the faith of the operation of God" (Col. 2:12).

The faith that a newly reborn sinner exercises in Christ immediately brings him into a state of justification. All his sins of every kind are pardoned in that instant. Christ, to whom he is now spiritually united, becomes his righteousness at once, thenceforth, and forever. God looks no more on the "filthy rags" of his unconverted state, but now sees him as "in Christ," who is the Lord our Righteousness.

In this sense, the sinner's "faith is counted for righteousness" (Rom. 4:5). This is why the dying thief, though before laden with guilt and sin, was at once fully pardoned and assured of a place that day in heaven (Luke 23:43). It is the same for all who believe in Christ: their death day is their day of entry into the glorious and happy presence of Christ.

The moment of our spiritual engrafting into Christ is the moment of our initiation into all the blessed benefits which the Lord Jesus has bought for us by His obedient life, His atoning death, and His triumphant resurrection. What Christ has done for us as believers becomes valid for us as believers subjectively. Two thousand years ago, the Son of God perfectly obeyed all God's laws in our nature for us, shed His blood on the cross for us, and rose again from the dead for us. These blessed actions of our Lord were done in time and they are objective and historical realities. But they have a subjective spiritual effect upon the soul of the person who believes in Him now, two thousand years later.

When the believer comes into union with Christ, the redemptive actions of Christ become true, in a subjective sense, in the spiritual condition of that believer. So, says Paul mysteriously, we "are dead to sin" (Rom. 6:2). "We are buried with him by baptism into death: that like as Christ was raised up from the dead by the glory of the Father, even so we also should walk in newness of life" (Rom. 6:4). Every real believer enters into this condition of walking "in newness of life" at his new birth. The soul of the newborn believer, in other words, has undergone a profound spiritual change in its relation with the realm of sin.

There is no denying the sense of amazement we feel when we read these words. But Paul is telling us what experience confirms every time. Those who come to Christ turn from sin and strive after holiness. Sin, once the sphere in which we all lived, is now an alien domain to us. We hate it and we shun it—not perfectly, but sincerely and systematically. Though in this life we do not come to moral perfection, yet we are told "reckon ye also yourselves to be dead indeed unto sin, but alive unto God through Jesus Christ our Lord" (Rom. 6:11). Sin, once our pleasure ground, is now seen as forbidden territory.

The converted man has a renewed will to say "No" to sin's enticements. He cries out to God for strength to refuse the allurements of this sinful world. Through the help of Christ's Spirit living in him, he treads underfoot the tempting thoughts he once welcomed. He rejoices and thanks God to find that now "sin shall not have dominion" over him. He is no longer "under the law, but under grace" (Rom. 6:14).

As soon as the soul is united to Christ, it enjoys alterations which are divinely ordained and which utterly alter his relation to God and to the world. He is justified, and so reconciled to God. He is adopted into God's family and has an entitlement to all the blessings of the members of God's family. He is indwelt by the Spirit of holiness, who begins a life-long process of sanctification in his soul. In this process, the believer is not passive but active. He is called on to "work out" his salvation "with fear and trembling" (Phil. 2:12). The nature of this activity is to strive with might and main to become holy "in all manner of conversation" (1 Pet. 1:15). The principal purpose of the Holy Spirit's indwelling is to conform us to the image of Christ.

The indwelling of Christ in the soul is registered in the believer's consciousness by a heart-warming influence of divine activity called the witness of the Spirit (Rom. 8:16). God has not left us in the darkness of uncertainty but has "sealed" us by His Spirit. The result is that we have the "firstfruits of the Spirit" (Rom. 8:23) in our hearts even here and now in this present life.

The effect of the indwelling Spirit in our hearts is that we instinctively feel, through the activity of Christ's Spirit in us, a yearning for the perfection which is to be ours when Christ, who is our life, returns in glory. The soul of a believer vibrates, as it were, because the blessed Holy Spirit touches the heartstrings within us. We inwardly feel and we outwardly exclaim, "Even so, come, Lord Jesus" (Rev. 22:20).

Reader, are these experiences yours, or is your religion cold, empty, unfeeling? Seek God with all your soul and these foretastes of glory will be yours, too!

7

Seated with Christ in Grace and Glory

Union with Christ lifts us above this world to a state of elevation enjoyed by none who are strangers to saving faith. The apostle Paul refers to this in the following words: "[God] hath raised us up together, and made us sit together in heavenly places in Christ Jesus" (Eph. 2:6). Such a statement, so far beyond all human deduction or expectation, is one that we could only know of as the result of inspired and God-given revelation.

It is clear that our position as those who are seated with Christ in the heavenly places results from being in vital union with Him. In other words, a consequence of our intimate relationship with the exalted and glorified Lord Jesus is that we who are believers are dignified with this elevated status. We are "in Christ Jesus" as we "sit together" in the heavenlies.

Paul refers several times to this elevated status into which Christ has brought us. He informs us that God has "blessed us with all spiritual blessings in

heavenly places in Christ" (Eph. 1:3). We read that
God's almighty power raised Christ "from the dead,
and set him at his own right hand in the heavenly
places" (Eph. 1:20). Further, we learn of "the principalities and powers in heavenly places" to whom is
now made known God's "manifold wisdom" by the
church (Eph. 3:10). Again, we are bidden to put on
"the whole armor of God" because we fight not with
"flesh and blood" but with "spiritual wickedness in
high places" (Eph. 6:12). Clearly, our union with
Christ has brought us into a sphere into which none
enter who are strangers to Christ and to our mystical
union in Him.

It may very well be that the same status is in
mind when we read in Scripture of some who "lived
and reigned with Christ a thousand years" (Rev.
20:4). This passage has sometimes been understood
to teach a future millennium. However, the context
makes it clear that these saints who live and reign
with Christ are not alive in this world but dead and
in the world of spirits. They are said to have been
"beheaded for the witness of Jesus, and for the word
of God" (Rev. 20:4). Their life and reign with Christ
is above, not on the earth.

Obviously, there is a difference between the reign
of those spoken of in Revelation 20 and those referred
to in Ephesians. The former are saints in heaven and
in glory; the latter are saints here on earth. However,
there is still a similarity in the status of both the living and the martyred saints. They all, whether in life

or death, are elevated to a status that places them above the world.

The truth enshrined in such passages of Scripture is extremely precious. To be united to Christ is to be raised up to a place and to a position far above this world. In life, we sit with Him in high places; in death, we go into the very glory itself. We sit with Him in heavenly places here, and we reign with Him hereafter.

That we are now, in this life, seated with Christ in heavenly places refers to a state of grace. There is status and elevation, but, alongside it, there is also warfare and conflict. As long as we remain in this present world, we must contend, wrestle, and fight against the powers of hell and of dark wickedness. The reference, clearly, is to the hosts of fallen angels whom we cannot see but against whom we must wage warfare using the spiritual and God-given weapons.

The Christian life, then, is one of elevation. Indeed, we may say, it is one in which we may look for elevation in three stages, or in three degrees. From his new birth to his death, the Christian is elevated to the "heavenly places" here and now in this life. Then, at his death, the Christian is further elevated to a position in which he lives and reigns with Christ a thousand years (see Rev. 20:4). This is referred to as the intermediate state.

In the intermediate state, the soul of believers is disembodied. The body is laid in the grave and remains there in a state of decay and decomposition—but is still united to Christ. The soul immediately leaves the body at death and enters into glory with Christ. The soul in this intermediate state is perfectly holy and sinless. It is beyond all toil or trouble, and out of the reach of all temptation and trial. The soul is now morally perfect. But it is incomplete in that it is disembodied.

The souls of believers in the intermediate state await the reunion with their own bodies. In this temporary condition, the soul shares in the triumph of Christ. This is the second aspect of the believer's elevation through union with its Lord and Savior. It is very decidedly a wonderfully blessed and happy state. The Apostle John declares, "Blessed and holy is he that hath part in the first resurrection: on such the second death hath no power, but they shall be priests of God and of Christ, and shall reign with him a thousand years" (Rev. 20:6).

The intermediate state will last until the end of time. Evidently, Satan and the powers of hell will put forth their uttermost strength at the end and will seek to make a last stand against God and His church: "When the thousand years are expired, Satan shall be loosed out of his prison, and shall go out to deceive the nations which are in the four quarters of the earth..." (Rev. 20:7–8). This last desperate act of concerted opposition to our blessed Lord, however, will prove unavailing. Though Satan and his forces of evil do all they can, they are met with overwhelming divine power.

The Scriptures express it in these words: "They [i.e. the powers of evil] went up on the breadth of the earth, and compassed the camp of the saints about, and the beloved city" (Rev. 20:9). The people of God are surrounded and threatened with annihilation—or, at least, they appear for one dread moment to be. But then—blessed be God!—there will be an intervention from heaven: "Fire came down from God out of heaven, and devoured them" (Rev. 20:9).

The church's ages-long conflict with the powers of hell is now at an end. The punishment of all Christ's enemies is unspeakably dreadful, but perfectly just: "The devil that deceived them was cast into the lake of fire and brimstone, where the beast and the false prophet are, and shall be tormented day and night for ever and ever" (Rev. 20:10).

Now, at last, the ancient prophecy will be completely fulfilled: "It shall bruise thy head, and thou shalt bruise his heel" (Gen. 3:15). Satan bruised our Lord on the cross, but our Lord's wound was not incurable. To be wounded in the heel is painful but not mortal. Our Savior rose again triumphant from the grave. And, at the end of time, as John's vision in Revelation 20 informs us, Satan will be bruised in the head. This is a fatal blow. Of this, Paul also speaks when he informs us: "The God of peace shall bruise Satan under your feet shortly" (Rom. 16:20).

This crushing blow upon Satan will be at the Second Coming of our Lord in glory. At the same time, Christ will send out His voice and summon all the dead from their graves, as He prophesied: "The hour is coming, in the which all that are in the graves shall hear his voice and shall come forth; they that have done good, unto the resurrection of life; and they that have done evil, unto the resurrection of damnation" (John 5:28 – 29). This summons from the grave will be the third and final exaltation of the people of God. It is the beginning of their eternal happiness in the final and perfect state of glorification.

In life, the believer is in a state of grace and, as such, he sits with Christ in "the heavenly places." In death, he reigns with Christ in the intermediate state of glory, perfect in soul, but without his body. In the day of Christ's Second Coming, he is raised up in the resurrection to glory. Body and soul are now reunited; his redemption in Christ is complete. He is in the final state of glory. Now his whole future eternity is to enjoy the presence and to feel the love of God in Christ to all ages, world without end.

No wonder the redeemed are taught in this life to bless God for their election and for all the love and favor which God has chosen to give us in uniting us by faith to His dear Son, the Lord Jesus Christ (Eph. 1:3)! No wonder the glorified saints in the intermediate state worship God with songs of thankfulness and of praise: "Worthy is the Lamb that was slain to receive power, and riches, and wisdom, and strength, and honour, and glory, and blessing" (Rev. 5:12)!

What those joys are which the redeemed people of God shall enjoy with Him in the final state of glory we can only reverently place among the mysteries still to be made known. Surely they are things which "eye hath not seen, nor ear heard, neither have entered into the heart of man." They are, however, "things which God hath prepared for them that love him" (1 Cor. 2:9). They have in part been revealed in God's Word; but what they are in full the great day will show.

8

Evidences of a Real Union with Christ

Nothing is as tragic as a false hope of heaven. Yet multitudes in all ages have lived and died in a false profession of faith in Christ. They have claimed to be in union and fellowship with the Son of God, yet all their lives have been deluded. So serious is the subject that it demands of all who claim to be Christians that they examine themselves to see if they really have what they claim to have.

It is not an exaggeration to say that self-deception on the part of religious people is more common than we might suppose. After all, Christ Himself gave this warning in a variety of ways. "If...the light that is in thee be darkness, how great is that darkness!" (Matt. 6:23). Here our Lord shows that our supposed grasp of gospel truth can be essentially false. If so, it is fatal.

How terribly true that is! Millions who at this hour hold to a false form of Christianity do so with complete assurance. Yet their whole position before

God is entirely false. They are not only in the dark as to the real gospel, but they make their darkness doubly dark by imagining it to be light.

How do we account for the fact that those who are not in union with Christ may imagine that they are in a right relationship with Him? The answer is because they are deceived. "If our gospel be hid, it is hid to them that are lost: in whom the god of this world hath blinded the minds of them which believe not" (2 Cor. 4:3–4). Herein consists the supremely terrible deceitfulness of sin: men may be confident of having fellowship with Christ and yet have nothing but "a lie in their right hand" (Isa. 44:20).

The Lord Jesus Christ did not conceal this truth from men. He issues this solemn reminder repeatedly in His preaching: men may be deceived in supposing themselves to be saved. Not only does Christ tear into the hypocrisy of the Pharisees and Sadducees; He also turns the spotlight of self-examination on His own twelve disciples to teach them the need to make sure they are genuinely right with God. "Have not I chosen you twelve, and one of you is a devil?" (John 6:70). "One of you shall betray me," says our Lord to them (John 13:21). In matters as extremely serious as the soul, it is not kindness to allow people to be under the lifelong delusion of being saved when they are still under the wrath of God.

The apostolic writers of the New Testament all have this same cautionary note. They encourage and comfort God's children but also sound a warning signal to those whose religion is not well grounded in a right relationship with Christ. Paul puts it most bluntly: "Know ye not your own selves, how that Jesus Christ is in you, except ye be reprobates" (2 Cor. 13:5). To those with a mere notional faith James can say, "Thou believest that there is one God; thou doest well: the devils also believe, and tremble" (James 2:19). John, pointing to a great practical test, declares, "If a man say, I love God, and hateth his brother, he is a liar" (1 John 4:20). Jude's language is extremely strong. "These are spots in your feasts of charity, when they feast with you, feeding themselves without fear..." (Jude 12).

Jude's language is a sure reminder to us that there is a healthy and a necessary "fear" which true believers have. This fear is entirely consistent with being in vital union with Christ; it is a sincere and a profound concern to be in a right relationship with Christ. "The fool rageth and is confident" (Prov. 14:16). This foolish confidence is nowhere more out of place than in the life of a gospel hypocrite, who has neither any true fellowship with the living God nor any idea of how blind he is.

Those, then, who are united to Christ need to look for evidences of this union in their own lives and in the lives of others professing faith in the gospel. This is not to suggest that we can read men's hearts as only God can do. Nor is it to discourage the weak in faith or to raise joyless fears in genuine believers who may be shy and retiring about their profession of trust in a Savior. However, so serious a subject is the relation of our soul to God that kindness compels us to press on one another, as Christians, the need to "search and try our ways." Painful self-examination which leads to real repentance is, after all, far preferable to a self-deceived, comfortable journey to hell.

Scripture offers many clear "marks" or evidences to indicate what sort of people we should be if we claim to be in union with the Son of God. We need to consider some of these "marks of grace," as we usually call them. Our concern is to see what sort of life we need to have if we wish to assure ourselves that we are truly "in Christ." John puts the issue in this way: "He that saith he abideth in him ought himself also so to walk as he [Christ] walked" (1 John 2:6).

This cannot possibly mean that believers must be as perfect as Christ was; rather, it means that a genuine child of God must have the same outlook on life as Christ had. Was Christ aiming at God's glory? So must we. Did Christ keep to God's moral law? So must we. Was our Lord regularly at prayer? So must we. Did He constantly speak about the truths of God to those around Him? Therefore, as far as we may, so should we seek to do. Did Christ experience the opposition of this world? So must Christians expect to find.

Those in real union with Jesus Christ are in this life not perfect. But they sincerely long after perfection and they grieve to come, as they know that they come, far short of God's standard in all things. Like Paul, the true believer cries out, "O wretched man that I am! who shall deliver me from the body of this death?" (Rom. 7:24). This is not the cry of the dissimulating hypocrite covering up before his fellow men for secret sins that he inwardly practices and delights in. It is the deeply sincere and heartfelt cry of anguish that a man in Christ utters all through his life here below because he never fully obeys the commandments of God, which he genuinely loves and approves of.

Sin has not only defiled us; it has disabled us. The man in Christ loves God and yearns to glorify Him by a life of perfect obedience. But "how to perform that which is good" he cannot discern (Rom. 7:18). The child of God in this world is like a disabled boy who watches an athletic event. He loves to see the running and jumping of those who are taking part. But, try as he might, he cannot do what they do. It is in his heart to be as fit and active as the athletes are, but a crippled body disables him. In his secret moments, he may shed tears to think how confined his poor body has made him in this life. Likewise, the man who is a real member of Christ's mystical body in this life sheds tears that he cannot keep the Ten Commandments. It is in his heart to be perfect. He wills to do God's will. He puts forth all his energies to please God. The desire is there, but the performance is at best far from perfect. He falls short of the conformity to God's revealed will he knows is his duty.

It might occur to us to ask a question when we consider this aspect of a Christian's life: "Are Christians not frustrated people if this inward conflict rages all the time?" The answer we give is, "Yes and no." Let me explain. The Christian life is a many-sided one. If the above aspect were the only one, it might well be true that every believer in Christ would be pitiable because he is always aware of the inward struggle of which we have spoken. But there are such comforts, consolations, and delights for the believer along with the frustrations that a believer often has an inward feast. This feast of happiness in the soul of every child of God arises from both knowledge and experience.

Union with Christ involves knowledge of what God has told us. He loves us and takes us for His own dear children. If, in this life, we are disabled children who cannot perfectly do what we wish to do in our obedience to God's revealed will, yet we are here and now God's cherished people. Here is a mighty comfort indeed—and we are able to add a further consolation. Soon, very soon, we shall be perfect in soul when we bid farewell to this world at death. More still, we know that, in the resurrection, our body will also be fully perfect and an ideal vehicle for our eternal enjoyment of God!

9

The Love of God to Those in Christ

Could any privilege be greater than that fallen and sinful creatures should be pardoned by the great God and brought into eternal fellowship with Himself in Christ? This is the privilege and honor that the Eternal has given to all who are in Christ. We might not be surprised to learn from God that He created angels and unfallen spirits to be eternally engrafted into Himself. But God did not choose to do so. Rather, He elected ruined and lost men and women to this high destiny. No wonder the prophets spoke ecstatically of this love of God and cried out, "Sing, O heavens; and be joyful, O earth" (Isa. 49:13). Again, "Sing, O daughter of Zion; shout, O Israel; be glad and rejoice with all the heart, O daughter of Jerusalem.... The Lord thy God in the midst of thee is mighty" (Zeph. 3:14, 17).

It is easy to believe that a great king could pardon rebels and show mercy to them in order to display his goodness and mercy. But God, who has certainly done all this, has done so much more. The gospel does not merely confer pardon on men. It gives them a privileged status above all other created beings: to be members of Christ's body throughout all ages to come—"of his flesh, and of his bones" (Eph. 5:30)! This is an exquisite truth, if anything ever was. It means that Christ will treat us as precious to Himself, near to Himself, dear to His heart, an object of eternal delight. As a wife is precious to her husband above all that he has, so will believers be to Christ. They are precious above all other created beings whatsoever. This honor is not given even to unfallen angels; they are "ministering spirits sent forth to minister for them who shall be heirs of salvation" (Heb. 1:14).

There are—and of necessity must be—profound mysteries surrounding this subject that our minds cannot begin to grasp in this life. But what we understand from the overall teaching of Scripture is sufficient to quicken our desire to understand how close our union with the blessed Son of God will be eternally in a better world.

There are at least three mysterious unions revealed to us in Scripture. There is the union of the three holy and glorious Persons in the Trinity. Secondly, there is the union of the two natures in the Person of Christ. Thirdly, we are told that believers are already in a union with Christ—a union that is to last forever.

What do we know from Scripture about each of these unions? Concerning the Holy Trinity, we are to believe that each Person is equally God. Each Person shares in the divine essence of the Godhead, and each Person indwells the others. This mutual indwelling, so far beyond our comprehension, is referred to by theologians as "circumincession." Each Person of the Godhead is filled with love for the other Persons and delights in them while maintaining a distinct relation to the other Persons. The Father eternally begets the Son. The Son is eternally begotten of the Father. And the Holy Spirit eternally proceeds from the Father and the Son. We refer to these distinctive operations as the "internal works" of God.

These internal works of God differ from the "external works" of God in important ways. The "internal works" of God are eternal, like God Himself, and depend not on God's will, but on His own character. The outward works are creation, providence, redemption, and judgment. These external works are all dependent on God's will and they will all glorify God's attributes eternally.

What a joy to see in the Bible how each of the divine Persons is full of love and kindness in reference to the other two Persons! For instance, we hear from the lips of God the Father this tribute to Christ at His baptism: "This is my beloved Son, in whom I am well pleased" (Matt. 3:17). The Father's voice confirms this same love to the Son at the transfiguration (Matt. 17:5). This love that the Father has for the Son and the beautiful, repeated expression of it are a reflection of the eternal complacency and delight that He, as the first Person of the Godhead, feels towards the second Person. It is a perfect pattern of how we who are "in Christ" and have spiritual fellowship with the Son of God should think and feel about the Lord Jesus.

Similarly, Christ loves the Father in an eternal and perfect love, which comes to expression in the Bible at various points. "Believe me that I am in the Father, and the Father in me" (John 14:11). "I and my Father are one" (John 10:30). The word "one" here is not masculine but neuter. It would perhaps suggest the thought of one God, one divine Being, not one Person. But nowhere perhaps do we see the love of the Son to the Father more perfectly expressed than in these words of Christ: "I have glorified thee on the earth: I have finished the work which thou gavest me to do" (John 17:4). The Father required in eternity past that Christ should take our nature and, in it, die on the cross for us sinners. O what an expression of love then on Christ's part that He will gladly drink the cup which the Father has given him (John 18:11)! That is love indeed.

The language of the Son of God always and in every way reflects His love for the Father. Indeed, we could well say that every item of teaching which Christ gives us is an outpouring of His own devotion to the honor and glory, the obedience and submission, owed to God the Father. In taking our nature, Christ owed to the Father all such obedience and reverence due in view of the commandment to love God with all our being. No man ever glorified or

loved God the Father so completely and entirely as
the incarnate Son of God in this world. In this, as in
all else, He is a perfect example of how we are to live
in unbroken fellowship with God and with an eye
always to the advancement of the Father's glory by
total submission to the Father's will.

There is the clearest evidence of love and honor
in all Christ's references to the Holy Spirit. One of
the striking statements of Christ is this: "Whosoever
speaketh a word against the Son of Man, it shall be
forgiven him: but whosoever speaketh against the
Holy Ghost, it shall not be forgiven him, neither
in this world, neither in the world to come" (Matt.
12:32). It is both a warning to blasphemers and
a beautiful, affectionate tribute to the honor and
esteem—yes, love and delight—which the Son of
God has in the third Person of the Godhead.

Conversely, the Spirit is full of love for the other
two Persons of the Godhead. Remarkably we are told
that He "will not speak of himself" but of Christ. His
work in this world, says Christ, is to "glorify me"
(John 16:14).

In a most perfect and harmonious union, the
three Persons are spoken of as having one great purpose in common, in which each perfectly performs
the part distributed to Him to do: "All things that
the Father hath are mine: therefore said I, that he
shall take of mine and shall show it unto you" (John
16:15). Such union of love between the Persons of the

one true and living God! What a place of harmony and of love will heaven be!

The second union we referred to is that of the two natures in the one Person. Theologians call this the "hypostatic union." Christ is God the Son; but in order to save His elect, He had to take their nature on Himself. The logic of this is clear. Man committed sin, so man must atone for sin. The wages of sin is death; therefore, to pay those wages, Christ had to assume our nature and die in it. It was absolutely necessary for Him to assume human nature into union with His eternal divine nature. As to His divine nature, He is equal to the Father and the Holy Spirit. As to His human nature, He has a body and soul as we do, and was like us in all respects except that He had no sin.

Jesus Christ, then, has these two perfect natures; but He is *one* Person. He has two minds (one human and so limited; the other omniscient) and He has two wills. In the divine mind, Christ knows everything; in the human mind, Christ is limited. Hence, we hear Him utter these words in reference to His second coming and the time of it: "But of that day and that hour knoweth no man, no, not the angels which are in heaven, neither the Son, but the Father" (Mark 13:32). It is clear that, insofar as Christ is man, He did not know the day or the hour; but, insofar as He is God and so one with the Father, He did know.

The third union of which we speak is the mystical union. This is the blessed relationship that all believers have with Christ when they come into a state of grace. The relationship will never end. Believers are to be forever in the blessed condition of being "in Christ."

This wonderful and inspiring truth is clear from many passages of Scripture, not least from the great High Priestly prayer of our Lord, where we hear Him uttering these words: "Father, I will that they also, whom thou hast given me, be with me where I am" (John 17:24).

Therefore, the mystical union by which Christ and His people are joined in an eternal relationship of blessedness and fellowship must go on unbreakable through life and, at last, bring us to perfect happiness and an enjoyment of celestial love. Of this wondrous state, our Savior speaks in the same passage: "That they may behold my glory, which thou hast given me: for thou lovedst me before the foundation of the world" (John 17:24). The heavenly state to which all who are in blessed union with Christ are to come will be one of eternally beholding His glory! And, with that high privilege, to enjoy Christ's love: "That the love wherewith thou hast loved me may be in them, and I in them" (John 17:26).

The devil's lie to our first parents was that, if they disobeyed God, they would be "as gods" (Gen. 3:5). God's unspeakable grace and love to us in Christ is to make us, as believers, the sons of God — and, as such, to enjoy eternal union with the Son of God Himself! O how God should be loved, adored, and praised, world without end!

10

The Unction that
Teaches Believers

Scarcely anything distinguishes those who are in Christ from all others more clearly than the attitude they, as believers, have to the Bible. The Lord, who unites us to Himself in a common spiritual life, imparts to those who are His a special influence of His Spirit by which all true believers recognize the divine origin and unique authority of the Bible as the Word of God.

Christ teaches His own to receive the Bible as their supreme authority in matters of faith and conduct by giving to them an "unction," or "anointing," which "teaches them all things." In a manner that we cannot fully explain, God's Spirit, given to us when Christ is ours, begins a lifelong work of education in religious knowledge. This the Spirit does, not without the means of grace, but through the means of grace. The believer's view of the Bible then becomes the exact same view as what Christ Himself had and has. We are inwardly taught and persuaded that the Scriptures are of divine origin, that they are inspired of God, and are authoritative. The child of God does not believe these things about the Bible because of any formal course of training or theological education; it is an inward conviction brought home to his consciousness by the inward testimony of God's Spirit.

The sad fact is that mere outward privilege or education in venerable institutions and biblical learning cannot of themselves create in us the certainty that the Bible is God's Word. Sad experience repeatedly proves that the privileged children of great theologians and preachers do not necessarily become sound in the faith. Too often, they reject the conservative view of their fathers for a liberal view of the Bible. It is not scholarship that leads liberal scholars to have low views of the Bible; the fact is that our natural pride and carnal wisdom are more than sufficient to make us reject the infallibility of the Bible. Those who are not "in Christ" do not have the "anointing" which is essential to a sound view of the Bible.

But when Christ unites us with Himself, He generates within our heart and mind a regard for the Bible identical to His own. For Christ, "It is written" puts an end to all controversy. This is so because, as our Lord expresses it, "the Scripture cannot be broken" (John 10:35). If doubt should remain, our Lord also affirms His total belief in the Bible's inspiration with words which can scarcely be misinterpreted: "Heaven and earth shall pass away: but my words shall not pass away" (Mark 13:31). This must be so because, as Jesus says in prayer to His Father, "Thy word is truth" (John 17:17).

The Bible will never be read, studied, or loved as it ought to be until men realize that it is the one and only "light that shineth in a dark place" (2 Peter 1:19). Therefore, in order that we might be sanctified by the truth of Scripture, Christ, in uniting us to Himself, gives to us the Spirit of illumination by which we recognize the Bible to be the infallible revelation of God.

In matters of religion, this anointing is of the highest importance. Men, even able and learned men, may immerse themselves in the study of religious subjects, but they will see nothing clearly until God opens their eyes with a supernatural illumination so that they come to sound and scriptural understanding. This is the force of Christ's warning to "beware of the leaven of the Pharisees and of the Sadducees" (Matt. 16:11). Even the apostles of Christ did not immediately understand this expression. However, they came to see that our Lord was warning them of two terribly dangerous mistakes in their handling of the Scriptures: to add to them or to take away from them. The Pharisees did the first; the Sadducees, the second. Both religious groups did so to their undoing.

History has abundantly shown the peril of not heeding this grave warning of Christ. Before the Reformation, Christianity in the Middle Ages became utterly corrupted because human traditions and church traditions were superimposed on the Word of God. The gospel was all but buried out of sight. It was the great mercy of God to give to the world the Reformation, by which the proper principle in religion was again, after long, dark centuries of error, recovered through the great teaching of our Protestant theologians, especially John Calvin.

But history since the Reformation has the same lesson to teach later. In the nineteenth century, the higher criticism emanating from Germany and flooding theological colleges and universities of other countries taught theological students to regard parts of the Bible as unreliable. In Britain and elsewhere, this liberal movement has led to terrible spiritual decline in the Christian churches and to terrible moral decline in society at large.

If we are in fellowship with Jesus Christ, we must reject all views of the Bible that are inconsistent with that of Christ and His apostles: "All Scripture is given by inspiration of God" (2 Tim. 3:16). The corollaries of this grand statement are that the Bible must be obeyed and believed as though we heard its words being spoken audibly from heaven every day we live here in this life. We must treat the Bible with reverential awe and fear. This is because we shall one day be judged by what we have done and how we have—or have not—believed and practiced all that it teaches.

The problem of fallen man does not end when he hears the gospel preached. His need is far more than a good preacher to tell him what God says. He also needs to have an inward disposition given him by which he will readily accept the truth of God's Word and apply himself conscientiously to the duty of doing what it says because it is God who is speaking to him in it.

This point is vividly illustrated in the life of two Old Testament kings of Judah: Josiah and Jehoiakim. When Josiah heard the Word of God read to him, he at once recognized the immense seriousness of what he heard and, in sorrow at the nation's sin, he rent his clothes and repented (2 Chron. 34:19). But Jehoiakim, on hearing the Word of God some years later, was so completely unmoved by its warnings and threatenings that he cast it, almost page by page, into the fire (Jer. 36:23).

The only way to account for this completely different reaction to God's words in the case of these two Jewish kings is to see that the one, Josiah, had spiritual union in his soul with Christ and so he "trembleth at my word" (Isa. 66:2). The other king, not having the unction of the Spirit on his soul, was deaf to God's voice; he treated with contempt what the Almighty was saying to him and to the whole nation. This he did to his own terrible hurt and eternal loss.

We see in these historical examples how much we in our day need to see a revival of God's grace in society at large. If people have Christ in their souls, they will also, like Josiah, tremble at the Word of God and be fearful for their souls and penitent for their sins. In days of revival, God gives to men a new sense of fear for their souls. This is because the Spirit of God convinces men of "sin, and of righteousness, and of judgment" (John 16:8). The Word preached becomes vividly personal. Men feel they are in need of salvation. They cry out, as on the Day of Pentecost, "What shall we do?" (Acts 2:37). Christ's voice is heard in the inmost heart and in the conscience. In a day of revival and blessing, Christ causes multitudes to fear for their own eternal safety. The agent through whom they come to realize their danger is the Holy Spirit. To those who come to Christ, the Spirit is given so that they feel the comforts of God's love and grace. Being now in spiritual union with Christ, they are blessed with the anointing which teaches all things (1 John 2:27).

Dear reader, do you have this unction in your own soul? God will give this to all who sincerely ask Him for it. The evidence that we have this unction is the same in all God's children: we love the Bible and hold fast to its blessed teachings all our life, until we enter, after death, into God's presence. There, at last, we will need His Bible no more.

11

Christ and His Church

Little as people of this world suppose, our highest privilege possible is to belong to the church of Christ. Of course, there are different senses in which we speak of the church. Here we refer to it as the body of believers in all ages who have believed in Christ as their Savior and Lord. The history of the church in this sense (which is the true meaning of the term "church") therefore spans all of history, and it will go on to span the years and ages to come until Christ, her blessed Lord, at last returns for her.

The church began in the Garden of Eden, when our first parents received the gospel's promise of a Savior who would one day come to destroy the work of the devil, who had just tempted them into their fallen state. Since then, the church has been growing as more and more believers have been added to it. The antediluvian patriarchs entered the church by faith in God's promise and they lived by faith during their long life in the world. So, too, the patriarchs after the Flood came into the church by faith in the

Christ whom they believed would one day come to save His people.

At the time of Abraham, God began largely to confine for a period the development of the church to one family of the earth. We refer to them as the Jewish race. From Abraham to Christ's day, the church was almost exclusively made up of Jews, though a small number of Gentiles, like Rahab and Ruth, were taken in by God. The vast majority of the families of the earth, for some two thousand years, were left to wander in ignorance of God. The church of that period was to be found alone among the children of Israel; it was a national church. But God made it clear early on that this national aspect of His church was only temporary. Even as early as the days of Abraham, God had stated that in him "shall all families of the earth be blessed" (Gen. 12:3). The day would come when God would gather to Himself all the nations — or, to speak more precisely, gather sinners to Himself out of all the nations on earth. That day came at Pentecost. From Pentecost to the present, God has been gathering sinners to Himself from an ever-widening number of countries and peoples.

God assures us in His Word that there will still be a future development. He informs us that the time will yet come when He will again bring the Jews back into the church. For two thousand years, the Jews as a people, apart from a small number in every age, have been cast off. But, we are assured by God, that He will one day "graft them in again" (Rom. 11:23). The engrafting here refers to the reception back into the true church of the Jewish people in great numbers.

God's ways are mysterious and past finding out, but they are all done in consummate wisdom and brought to pass with infallible certainty. Over the course of history, nations and kingdoms have come and gone, risen and fallen. Empires come and go. But God's church is steadily and certainly growing in the earth. Thus, those who belong to Christ's church belong to the one institution on earth that will remain throughout history. To speak of a "post-Christian" age is to speak ignorantly; the church of Christ is as sure to outlast all empires as she is sure at last to enter the "new heavens and new earth" (2 Peter 3:13).

But we must be clear what we mean by the "church" of God. We do not speak of some religious organization, however venerable or ancient. The biblical definition of the church is that it is made up of all and only those men and women in this world who are spiritually united to Christ as their Savior and Lord. This privilege can only be enjoyed when we have repented of our sins and have become "one" with Christ. The safety and permanence of the church is guaranteed by its being built on Christ. Our Lord referred to this great truth when He stated that He would build His church on a rock and the gates of hell would not prevail against it (Matt. 16:18). The "rock" is Christ and all that body of truth He has given us in the Bible.

There is no doubt that this is the correct interpre-

tation of Christ's words. Both Paul and Peter confirm
it for us. Paul affirms: "Other foundation can no man
lay than that is laid, which is Jesus Christ" (1 Cor.
3:11). This makes clear the identity of the church's
foundation. Paul puts it elsewhere in these words:
"[Believers] are built upon the foundation of the
apostles and prophets, Jesus Christ himself being
the chief corner stone" (Eph. 2:20). Peter explains
the same truth in similar terms: "To whom coming
[i.e. Christ], as unto a living stone, disallowed indeed
of men, but chosen of God, and precious, ye also, as
lively stones, are built up a spiritual house, an holy
priesthood, to offer up spiritual sacrifices, acceptable
to God by Jesus Christ" (1 Peter 2:4 – 5).

The church, then, is God's temple built on the
person and work of Christ. Believers are in a spiritual
union with Him. Each particular believer, like a stone
in God's temple, has his or her special place in the
purpose of God. This temple has been growing over
the many centuries of mankind's history; first came
our fallen parents, then the early patriarchs, then the
Jewish forefathers and those of Israel who believed.
After the great outpouring of the Spirit at Pentecost
came the Gentile believers. Therefore, the church will
grow by God's grace until all those who are eternally
His are brought safely in. Then, when the church is
complete, Christ will return to take her to glory.

It is a sad misreading of the Bible to suppose that
Christ's church is a mere religious society of persons
outwardly bound together by an interest in services

of worship, or even merely by the sacraments of baptism and the Lord's Supper. The essence of church membership is a person's spiritual union with Christ. This union is not present in anyone's life until he or she is born again by the power of the Holy Spirit and so brought into a vital relationship with Christ.

Christ Himself uses a variety of illustrations to make the point very clear: "The water that I shall give him shall be in him a well of water springing up into everlasting life" (John 4:14). This is a figurative way of saying that we need to have Christ's Holy Spirit in our souls. The Spirit alone can give us the life of grace — and that Spirit is only received when we come to Christ. Again, our Lord puts it this way: "The hour is coming, and now is, when the dead shall hear the voice of the Son of God: and they that hear shall live" (John 5:25). Those who are real Christians have heard Christ's voice in the gospel and they have had a spiritual resurrection. They are now united to Christ in the life of grace. Again, to the amazement of the hearers, Christ puts it like this: "Except ye eat the flesh of the Son of man, and drink his blood, ye have no life in you" (John 6:53). The meaning of our Lord, as before, is this: we must be in a relationship of spiritual union with Christ by which He supplies grace to our souls every day of our life here on earth. It is a mistake to refer these words to the Lord's Supper; the sacrament did not exist at this time. Christ is telling us of our need to be "in him" and "feeding on him." Without such a relationship with Him, a man has no spiritual life. And Christ tells us again: "If a man keep my saying, he shall never see death" (John 8:51). The true believer, being in union with Christ, receives all Christ's teachings and is an heir of everlasting life. No man can believe what Christ teaches until he has the Spirit of Christ in his soul.

Religious men may be outwardly devout, but they are in darkness until they believe savingly in Jesus. Our Lord makes this point forcibly to the unbelieving Pharisees: "For judgment I am come into this world, that they which see not might see; and that they which see might be made blind" (John 9:39). The merely religious man who has no spiritual union with Christ becomes judicially hardened by his self-righteousness and pride. This hardness entails religious blindness to the gospel. It was for this reason that deeply religious men crucified their own Messiah. On the other hand, when a humble, contrite sinner believes in Jesus as Lord, he or she at once receives a place in the church of God. Such believers are at once pardoned and brought into the enjoyment of God's love. Dear reader, are you genuinely and sincerely a believer in Christ? If so, how great is your privilege!

12

The Blessed Fellowship
of Believers in Christ

Those who are united with Christ are also spiritually united with all who are in Him. As the Lord and
His church are "one" (John 17:11, 21), so believers
who are engrafted into Christ are also one in heart
and mind with one another. Scripture says that they
are branches in the "true vine" (John 15:1f), "living
stones" in the same spiritual temple (1 Pet. 2:5), and
members of His body, "of his flesh and of his bones"
(Eph. 5:30).

Because of indwelling sin and as the result of
their varying degrees of knowledge and understanding, believers may differ in this world in many ways.
Yet they have a special regard for all who share their
faith and who profess Christ as their Lord and Master.
Scripture says that this common bond of love is necessary: "Whosoever believeth that Jesus is the Christ is
born of God: and every one that loveth him that begat
loveth him also that is begotten of him" (1 John 5:1).
To love God is to love those who share our status as

children of God's family. After all, we have one faith and one Father.

Much is made in Scripture of this blessed fellowship that all believers have with one another in the Lord. It is the basis of exhortations to maintain and promote love, like-mindedness, and unity one with another in this present life. Our Lord warns against a temptation in the human heart to elevate ourselves above one another: "Be not ye called Rabbi: for one is your Master, even Christ; and all ye are brethren" (Matt. 23:8). Again, says our Lord, "Neither be ye called masters: for one is your Master, even Christ" (Matt. 23:10). The same use is made by Paul of this relationship of being brethren in the Lord: "Walk worthy of the vocation wherewith ye are called, with all lowliness and meekness, with longsuffering, forbearing one another in love; endeavoring to keep the unity of the Spirit in the bond of peace. There is one body" (Eph. 4:1–4).

Christians, however much they differ in gifts, understanding, or sanctification, are one in all the main things: "One Lord, one faith, one baptism, one God and Father of all, who is above all, and through all, and in you all" (Eph. 4:5–6). This unity is not merely, or even mainly, external; it is a unity of spiritual life and fellowship with God through faith in Jesus Christ. The existence of many denominations of the visible church does not destroy this unity. The unity still exists—provided those who profess faith in Christ do so as a result of the new birth and not merely from cultural or other insufficient reasons.

The unity of true believers transcends all boundaries of race or color. In Christ, all are one. "There is neither Greek nor Jew, circumcision nor uncircumcision, Barbarian, Scythian, bond nor free" (Col. 3:11). "There is neither male nor female: for ye are all one in Christ Jesus" (Gal. 3:28). "For by one Spirit are we all baptized into one body, whether we be Jews or Gentiles, whether we be bond or free; and have been all made to drink into one Spirit" (1 Cor. 12:13). All external differences sink into the background among those who have come into a saving relationship with the Lord Christ.

The lessons from these passages of Scripture are plain enough. When tempted to overstrain their distinctives over against other denominations, Christians must keep in mind that they have more areas of agreement than of disagreement. What Christians of different churches hold in common is greater than those things in which they differ. To hold Christ as our Head in reality and in truth is to be part of a great spiritual kingdom in which we share all that is vital with one another. Provided our union with Christ is the result of a saving experience of His power and grace, we belong to one another as brothers and sisters in a sense higher even than that of natural siblings.

In a striking incident recorded in the Gospels, our Savior is informed that His brothers and His mother were standing outside the crowded room and were calling to Him. Of those in the room who were waiting on His ministry our Lord asked, "Who is my mother, or my brethren?" He then exclaimed, "Behold my mother and my brethren! For whosoever shall do the will of God, the same is my brother, and my sister, and mother" (Mark 3:34–35). Christ is declaring that spiritual relationships take precedence over natural ones. He regards as His "brethren" all who obey the gospel's call to come to Him and to worship God (Heb. 2:11–13).

The church is made up of men and women then who belong to one another as heirs of the same promise in Christ. They have unity in the faith, being engrafted into Christ. They have a God-ordained diversity of gifts and of talents. Hence, we are to look upon the church as remarkable in these two ways: for unity and for diversity. The diversity has respect to the specific calling and function which each member of Christ's mystical body is called on in this life to exercise. The gifts and talents vary in their nature and in their size, but God sovereignly gives all so that believers in this life might be a blessing and a help to one another.

In this context, the Apostle Paul writes, "There are diversities of gifts, but the same Spirit. And there are differences of administrations, but the same Lord. And there are diversities of operations, but it is the same God which worketh all in all" (1 Cor. 12:4–6). Gifts of preaching, teaching, writing, or lecturing on God's Word are examples of what Paul has in mind.

No gift of God is given for self-advertisement. All is given by God for the profit of His people. We should thank God and use the gifts we may be given.

At this point, several mistakes may be made. Through indwelling sin, we may use our God-given gift for self-promotion rather than for the edifying of our brethren. But to do so is to betray immaturity and carnality on our part. Another error we may fall into in the matter of spiritual gifts is to expect the gifts given in the early church to be given in the church of today. We had better make sure that we are not pretending to have "gifts" which we do not really and genuinely possess. Are those who claim to "speak in tongues" really doing so—or are they uttering syllables with no meaning so as to impress others who hold to the same theory of the permanence of the "gifts" of the New Testament age? A further mistake in the use of gifts is to allow ourselves to become discouraged if we feel we have fewer gifts than our fellow-believers have. Paul shows that this is a misuse of God's gifts: "The body is not one member, but many. If the foot shall say, Because I am not the hand, I am not of the body; is it therefore not of the body?" (1 Cor. 12:14–15). The less-gifted member of the Christian community is precious and beloved, notwithstanding his lack of giftedness; he is one of God's elect people who will at last "shine forth as the sun in the kingdom of the Father" (Matt. 13:43).

The unity in faith and love is paramount in all our relationships one with another as the people of

God. So far as it is consistent with truth and with good conscience towards God, we should strive hard after unity with all who hold to Christ and show it by their submission to the supreme authority of the Bible. So Scripture says, "Endeavouring to keep the unity of the Spirit in the bond of peace" (Eph. 4:3).

Our duty to seek to preserve unity ceases as soon as men depart from the theology of God's inspired Word. Whatever grandiose claims people make for "their church" or for "their way of worshipping God," we are not at liberty to have spiritual fellowship with them if they adhere to serious error or reject central doctrines of God's Word. To claim that Bible-believing Christians should unite into one organization with those who reject the sole and the sufficient authority of the Bible as God's revelation to man is to argue that light should have fellowship with darkness (see 2 Cor. 6:14). We might then argue that Christ and the apostles should have united with the Pharisees and Sadducees to form a mega-church, rather than forming what we know as the New Testament apostolic church of Jesus Christ.

The crucial factor in ecumenical relations, as in most other relations, is this: Do those with whom we propose to unite hold to the truth in love? If they do not, there cannot be any unity in the New Testament sense of that term. When Christ prays that His people may be "one," He refers to oneness in their union with Himself and not to mere organizational unity (John 17:21).

The blessed fellowship, which true believers enjoy with one another here below, is the foretaste of a higher and more perfect fellowship of all the saints in glory at last. If our fellowship is sweet here below, in spite of our indwelling sin and our imperfect understanding of the Bible, how much sweeter it will be at last! There, in the "new heaven and new earth" all the elect, being now clothed in their resurrection bodies, will "follow the Lamb whithersoever he goeth" (Rev. 14:4). They "shall hunger no more, neither thirst any more" (Rev. 7:16). There, with the blessed Triune God as their supreme and exquisite delight, the elect will "rest from their labours" (Rev. 14:13). At long last, after centuries of labor and conflict, God's dear people will enjoy full and perfect fellowship with one another and with their Lord. "Their works do follow them" (Rev. 14:13). In these words, the Bible speaks of the reward which their good works will at last have from God. So the "end" will, for the people who love God, be the beginning of a happiness which "eye hath not seen nor ear heard, neither [hath] entered into the heart of man" (1 Cor. 2:9). In a word, they will "reign for ever and ever" (Rev. 22:5).

13

The Brotherly Bond
of Christian Love

Those who are united to Christ in the union of the Spirit are also united to one another in the bond of Christian love. As believers are certain of their eternal union with Christ, so they are also sure of their fellowship one with another, both in time, and in eternity to come. "Every one that loveth him that begat loveth him also that is begotten of him" (1 John 5:1). To be a real Christian means that we have a love for all the people of God who share our Christian faith. The love believers have for one another is not the result of being in the same church necessarily, nor of being committed to the same creed or confession. Experience teaches that we sometimes find ourselves closer to those of a different church than we are to some who are in our own. People vary in the degree of their spirituality. Some are better than their creed; others are committed to a creed in theory more than in practice.

We should shun weak and poor theology, but we should be ready to count as true Christian brothers and sisters those who clearly manifest the fruits of the Spirit in their personal lives. There will be many surprises in heaven. It behooves us to speak charitably of all who hold to Christ and to the Bible with real sincerity and faith. Christians all speak the same "language" when they have experienced the new birth. They all hold to the belief that Jesus Christ is the Son of God and the only Savior of men. Their faith is God-given and leads them to treat the Bible as the reliable and inspired Word of God. They may differ a great deal in the measure of their understanding of God's Word, but they recognize and receive it for what it is.

This said, we need to add that it is most important for believers that they be well taught and well instructed in the doctrines and practice of God's Word. Theology is most important for sanctification and service. But we must always be charitable in our estimation of those who are weak in theological understanding. If in knowledge they are "babes" (1 Cor. 3:1), it does not mean that they have no real fellowship with Christ. Rather, it shows that they have not had the privilege of gifted preachers and teachers, as others perhaps have.

There is a great ministry to be done among real believers who are still "babes" in Christ. Since they are one with Christ, we owe it to them to seek to feed their souls with better teaching than they have had. "Feed my lambs," said our blessed Savior to Peter (John 21:15). The worst thing that can happen to us if we are well taught in the Word of God and in doctrine is to allow in ourselves an aloof attitude to those whose grasp of the truth is still only feeble. To give a warm handshake to a weak brother and to introduce some good book of divinity may bless his soul immensely. We should remember how Aquila and Priscilla, by their affectionate action, advanced the understanding of the gifted and eloquent Apollos. Though he was "mighty in the scriptures" (Acts 18:24), yet he needed someone to "expound unto him the way of God more perfectly" (Acts 18:26). The good example of these dear believers, Aquila and Priscilla, should not be lost on us. By their brotherly action, they made a good man still better.

The bond of Christian love and fellowship can be periodically weakened and strained, but it cannot be broken. In all sorts of ways and at different times, we may have to disagree with our beloved brethren in the Lord. This is especially true when the doctrines and principles of God's Word are at stake. We must not suffer our brother to sin but by all means rebuke him (see Lev. 19:17.) It is not a duty of the Christian life to keep silent when our brethren go wrong. The way of Christian love is to seek to put our brother right. Paul acted on this principle when he wrote concerning Peter, "I withstood him to the face because he was to be blamed" (Gal. 2:11). If the rest of church history teaches anything, it shows that equally conscientious believers at times disagree strongly over their understanding of God's Word and on how to apply it to church life. This is to be expected because in this life we "know in part" (1 Cor. 13:19). Wrong notions and semi-scriptural theories are constantly arising in men's minds. But they are to be resisted and corrected by sound teaching. When necessary, those who advance strange theories need to be rebuked; but love and patient teaching may be a far better corrective than to heap a ton of bricks on men's heads. Does not Paul, ever zealous for truth, remind us of this when he writes, "In meekness instructing those that oppose themselves: if God peradventure will give them repentance" (2 Tim. 2:25)? After all, we are the servants of Christ, and "the servant of the Lord must not strive; but be gentle unto all men, apt to teach, patient" (2 Tim. 2:24).

Love, kindness, forbearance, and patience are all great virtues and they are to be encouraged in all circles where Christians gather for worship and fellowship. Just as some are born shortsighted and others are born farsighted, so among those who have Christ as Savior, some see truth clearly, and others less so. The fact remains that those who see less clearly always see the main things clearly enough.

Those who are in union with the blessed Redeemer agree on the great essentials: the Trinity, the Godhood of Jesus Christ, the universality of sin, the need of repentance and faith, the reliability of the Bible, the reality of heaven and hell. All who have a real union with Christ see these things and believe heartily in them. Where men cast doubt on these fundamental truths, there is no real faith and no vital union with Christ. It is the great work of Christ as our Prophet to teach His people the essentials.

It is our comfort to know that all the Lord's people will, in heaven, at last see "eye to eye" (Isa. 52:8). "Then shall I know even as also I am known" (1 Cor. 13:12). But that happy degree of knowledge has not yet arrived. We are still in a state of grace, and a state of grace is not a state of glory. In heaven, the believer's understanding will be perfected, even as his body and soul will be. No darkness will remain. In Christ's presence, all who are His shall perfectly agree on every article of the creed to which they hold.

It is a pity that good men have sometimes gone to war against one another in this life because they have differed somewhat over their understanding of the truths of God's Word. We need to distinguish between infirmity and perversity. Children of God, through infirmity, may cling to some eccentric views of the truth, but we must remember, before we launch a hail of rockets at them, that we are to spend eternity with them. Infirmity in God's people can surely be dealt with by gentler weapons than incendiary bombs or scud missiles. If men are right in the main things, let us treat them with the courtesy befitting all our dealings with them. After all, they are Christ's people.

Perverseness is different. If errorists and heretics, after due correction, adhere still to their bold and daring falsehoods, we must look upon them and treat them as not true Christians. "A man that is an heretic after the first and second admonition reject;

knowing that he that is such is subverted, and sinneth, being condemned of himself" (Titus 3:10 – 11). Therefore, those who add their own religious books to the Bible as an additional source of revelation are not Christian believers. Those who hold to some view of God other than the Trinity; who deny the deity of Christ; or who reject the atonement, the virgin birth, or the resurrection of Christ are not real Christians, whatever claim they may make. They have not been taught by Christ's Spirit. They do not belong to Him.

What a blessing it is to have the fellowship of like-minded brothers and sisters in the Lord in this life! How much sweeter life is with them in our circle of our friends! Their company cheers us along this pilgrim journey. Their experiences of Christ enrich us. Their conversation edifies us. Their counsel guides and restrains us.

Christ's church is a flock. They go through the "valley of the shadow of death," not singly, but collectively. The Lord's flock "lie down in green pastures... and beside still waters" (Psalm 23:2). Many a time, were we left by Christ to go alone through life's trials, our hearts would faint and fail us. But we are not on our own, thanks to God's wise arrangement. We who are united here to Christ have brothers and sisters "an hundredfold" (Matt. 19:29). What Christian, however eminent for gifts or usefulness, has not been indebted to others who have been used by God for his or her good, along the journey to the Celestial City? Not Augustine, who so valued his dear friend

Alypius. Not Luther, whose soul was so refreshed by Melanchthon's company. Not Calvin, who owed so much under God to the fiery challenge of William Farel, through whose threatening words he remained in Geneva to help the cause of Christ there—and all over the world.

Dear reader, if you love Christ, love also all His people. If they are born from above and are in union with Him as their Head, then do all you can to promote their spiritual and their eternal good.

14

Fellowship with Christ in His Sufferings and Joys

Fellowship is a bond that binds together those who have a common outlook and common ideals. In every family, when one member sorrows, all the other members are made sad. When one member rejoices, as at a marriage or at a child's birth, all the family members enter into the other's joy. In its very nature, union is a bond that touches our sympathies and affects our emotions.

This principle of emotional sympathy is equally present in all who are at one with Christ in the mystical union we have as believers with Him. To believe in Jesus and to love Him is to be made glad when He is honored and sad when He is scorned. This is not mere "party spirit." Christians do not act merely like a political lobby or pressure group because of some common objective concerning their outward advantage. They feel it personally and keenly when their Lord and Master is referred to with disrespect. Conversely, they are made glad when they see Him respected, believed in, and magnified. Love weeps with those who weep and rejoices with those who rejoice, as the apostle enjoins us to do (Rom. 12:15).

This principle of sympathy can only be accounted for as a fruit of affectionate attachment. In a relationship of love, we instinctively desire the well-being of the other person. We are jealous of the name and reputation of those with whom we are united in the bond of affection. This is reflected in the Bible in all sorts of ways; one very strong expression of it is to be found in these words: "Do not I hate them, O Lord, that hate thee?... I count them mine enemies" (Ps. 139:21–22).

The Psalmist does not mean that, because he loves God, he intends to go about harming all who do not share his love of God. He knows that it is the believer's duty to "love thy neighbour as thyself" (Lev. 19:18). How then can the Psalmist allow himself to speak of "hating" God's enemies—"I hate them with perfect hatred: I count them mine enemies" (Ps. 139:22)? These strong words are used to convey his zeal for God's honor and his disapproval of all speech or conduct that would be offensive in God's sight. This "hatred," then, is the index of his jealousy for the name and reputation of God. He never treats these enemies with anything but love and kindness because the God whom he loves demands of us that we love our enemies and do good to them (Luke 6:35). But he is deeply hurt by their careless and irreverent attitude to God.

To be in union and fellowship with God means that we share in the attitudes and judgments which we see to be in God and in Christ, as these attitudes and judgments are revealed to us in the Bible. At the Flood, we see that God was deeply displeased by the lawless and barbarous behavior rampant on the earth at that decadent age of mankind: "It repented the Lord that he had made man on the earth, and it grieved him at his heart" (Gen. 6:6). The proof of our union in grace with God is that, in any similar age of violence and irreligion, as God's people, we, too, grieve to see or hear of the criminal behavior in society. This grief on the part of believers is not put on just to impress the onlooker. It is the true believer's genuine and inevitable inward pain when he hears of lawlessness in society. He instinctively shares the same reaction as reflected in the above text: It grieved God to his heart. Sin and crime are things that ought not to be. They ought not to exist. It is painful to a godly man to hear of the evidence and the incidence of such things in God's world for which God has expressed His holy repugnance.

Similarly, the believer is grieved when he meets religious superstition or ignorance in any society. This is seen in the soul of the Apostle Paul as he walked through pagan Athens and saw the visible evidence of their idolatry. We read that Paul's "spirit was stirred in him, when he saw the city wholly given to idolatry" (Acts 17:16). This "stirring of spirit" in Paul was a profound spiritual grief at the guilty ignorance betraying itself in the abominable statues and altars to imaginary gods all over the city of Athens.

To be in union with Christ entails similar emotions in God's people today. Though the outward forms of the idolatry of modern society are different, yet in its essence they are just as grievous to a seriously minded child of God. All conduct that does not respect God's being, will, and attributes of holiness and majesty is morally repugnant to everyone who walks with God. This is not to say that the believer is a "kill-joy"; it means that he cannot take pleasure in any event, however well patronized, which would be offensive in God's sight.

The union we have with God in a state of grace involves us as believers in having a compassionate view of the lost state of men and women all around us in this fallen world. We are not left in ignorance of Christ's inner feelings as He walked through the towns and cities of that day: "But when he saw the multitudes, he was moved with compassion on them, because they fainted, and were scattered abroad, as sheep having no shepherd" (Matt. 9:36). It is no different today. Mankind has not changed. The crowds walk up and down, searching for something to enjoy and to satisfy them. But they are tragically ignorant—indeed, in lands where the gospel has long been preached, many in society are culpably ignorant of where true life and peace are to be found. This is a melancholy spectacle to every serious child of God. We would dearly love to have the multitudes brought to know our blessed Savior and to have His joy in their lives.

As we share with Christ in His sorrowful reactions to the sad predicament of mankind in this world, we also share in the joy and gladness of Christ at the successes and advances of His gospel in this world. Christ's mission in coming into this world was "to seek and to save that which was lost" (Luke 19:10). Every time a sinner is brought to salvation, therefore, joy shall be in heaven (Luke 15:7) and "joy in the presence of the angels of God" (Luke 15:10). It is heaven's delight to see one lost sinner come to put his or her faith in Christ for salvation.

The saving of precious immortal souls is a work of incalculable importance to Christ. Though ten thousand sinners reject His message and are culpably blind to His loving overtures of salvation, yet our Lord will rejoice to have His elect children gathered safely into the fold: "I thank thee, O Father, Lord of heaven and earth, because thou hast hid these things from the wise and prudent, and hast revealed them unto babes" (Matt. 11:25). The gospel's offer is free to all who hear it; woe to those who reject or else despise it! But happy are all who welcome Jesus as their Lord and Master! Christ's joy is to have men and women weep their way to His feet and fall in love with Him for His unspeakable goodness to us. This joy is seen in Christ as He assures the penitent woman: "Thy faith hath saved thee; go in peace" (Luke 7:50).

To be united to Christ in the bond of eternal life is

to esteem His fellowship more precious than all else in the world: "Thy love is better than wine" (Song 1:2). This is why the Apostle Paul exclaims: "For me to live is Christ" (Phil. 1:21). Or again: "I am crucified with Christ: nevertheless I live; yet not I, but Christ liveth in me: and the life which I now live in the flesh I live by the faith of the Son of God, who loved me, and gave himself for me" (Gal. 2:20). Here is a mysterious statement indeed! It is the testimony of a man who is crucified, yet who lives, but who lives not his own life—for it is Christ who lives in him—and yet, he still lives after all because of a faith that unites him to the Son of God!

So wonderful is the union that every believer has with God's dear Son! No wonder the believer's emotions of sorrow and joy are profoundly roused by what he experiences in this life. He is not what he once was. The city of his soul now has another King ruling and governing it: "Christ in you, the hope of glory" (Col. 1:27).

Let evil men beware how they treat Christ's dear people. They are extremely precious to our risen and exalted Lord. They are the members of His body: "He that toucheth you toucheth the apple of his eye" (Zech. 2:8). Whoso raises his voice or his hand to smite Christ's children will answer to Him for it. Amazing is the nearness with which our Lord describes His relationship to His suffering people. This is made clear at Christ's appearance to Saul of Tarsus: "why persecutest thou *me*?" (Acts 9:4). Saul might have expected our Lord to speak of his persecuting *them*. But no! Wonderful union exists between the Lord of glory and His suffering and persecuted people below. Our Savior says, "Why persecutest thou *me*?" This is nearness indeed! Those who smite the Lord's dear people with tongue or pen, hand or fist, must stand before the almighty Son of God sooner or later.

15

Our Communion with Christ in Joyous Experiences

Our union with Christ is a permanent and unchanging relationship. It will not be broken by any power or influence within us or outside of us. It has the nature of a marriage contract, in which God in Christ proclaims the security of our status. "Thy Maker is thine husband" (Isa. 54:5). God divorces none that are in union with Him through the Mediator.

The security of our relationship is reaffirmed in that it is an "everlasting covenant" (Heb. 13:20). The end of time itself and the advent of "the new heavens and new earth" will not make void God's promise to be our God forever and ever. "The mountains shall depart, and the hills be removed; but my kindness shall not depart from thee, neither shall the covenant of my peace be removed" (Isa. 54:10). God proclaims His love to believers to be unbreakable: "I am married unto you" (Jer. 3:14).

Such assurances are exquisitely sweet and reassuring to those who have Christ as their one hope and as their crown of rejoicing. The hypocrite, who secretly savors sin while he hides his habits from others, may imagine that he has the best of both worlds. But he cannot know the pure happiness and innocent comfort that genuine believers have when they contemplate their privilege: to have Jesus Christ to all eternity. "The hypocrite's hope shall perish" (Job 8:13). The sweet sins that he rolls round his mouth now as he lives a lie will one day burn his flesh like fire. His religion is a tissue of deceits and he will lose all his joys when at last he loses his soul. What comfort now has Cain, Balaam, or Judas Iscariot? Though in this life they had a tincture of religion, it was but the thin veneer for a gnawing covetousness. Their real appetite was for this world, not for fellowship with the invisible God. Like the fool, they each reached out their hands for life's shadows and life's bubbles — for things of no substance.

But the true child of God has both union and communion with Christ. There is a difference between union and communion: union is permanent, communion is variable. Union does not alter, communion rises and falls. It waxes and wanes, like the seasons of the moon. Communion refers to the degree of our *felt* enjoyment of Christ's love for us in this world. In heaven at last, our communion with Christ will be as perfect and unvarying as our union now is, but in this life, it is variable. Factors are at work here in this life which cause our sense of Christ's love to rise and fall. Our joy is not always at high water mark.

Our love for Christ, never in this life perfect, is sometimes shamefully lukewarm (Rev. 3:16). The true reason for failure of affection on our part towards Christ is our indwelling sin and depravity. Our deceitful hearts may go out after the things of this world for a season—sometimes, even, after forbidden things. So we see in the lives of some of God's true people, both in Scripture and in history. Indeed, we all know by sad experience that our sense of desire for fellowship with Christ can grow weak, sometimes indeed very weak. Alas, we at times offer to our blessed Savior a very cold affection. Prayer is formal. Service is routine. Bible teaching is academic. Worship is wearisome. God forgive us that we at times sink to that dread state in which we have little more than "a name that thou livest" while in reality our souls are scarcely better than "dead" (Rev. 3:1). At such times, we must call ourselves to attention. When we are dry, dull, and unfeeling in our attachment to the Lord Jesus, we need to repent. It is imperative at such a time that we "be watchful, and strengthen the things that remain, that are ready to die" (Rev. 3:2).

In practical terms, this means that we must take steps to return to that condition of soul in which we have a felt sense of God's love and a faith that issues in holy emotions of delight in God. Our privilege, as those who are united to Christ, is so very great that, in a dull time of soul, we must adjust and alter our lifestyle so that we spend more time in things which most benefit the soul. The Word of God, prayer in secret, fellowship with lively believers—these are what we so much need when we no longer feel able to say genuinely "for me to live is Christ" (Phil. 1:21).

It is utterly wrong to think that we can allow ourselves to have faith without feelings, or that faith without feelings is sufficient. To suppose that a cold, intellectual faith is good enough contradicts so much that is told us in the Word of God. Such a faith at best may bring us to heaven. But, even at best, it will not give much glory to God or much joy to us in this life. At worst, such faith is no faith at all and it may let us down altogether in the day of death and of judgment.

If we aim to have an abundant entrance into the everlasting kingdom of our Lord and Savior Jesus Christ (2 Peter 1:11), we must "give diligence to make our calling and election sure" (2 Peter 1:10). Among the duties required to this end is the need to take due steps to keep ourselves in a "felt sense" of Christ's love for us. Nothing about us is as precious to Christ as our heart's affection for Him and our appreciation of Him as our Lord and Savior. He says to each believer as He said to Simon Peter, "Lovest thou me?" (John 21:15). Nothing stirs our own love for Christ so much as when we are conscious of His love for us: "God forbid that I should glory, save in the cross" (Gal. 6:14). If we take our eyes off the cross, our heart will go in search of other lovers. The way of recovery is to put right what we have done wrong: we need to kneel before a crucified Lord and receive

a fresh sense of what He has done for us: "Is it nothing to you, all ye that pass by?" (Lam. 1:12). "All that
Christ did, He did for me," let us say to ourselves.
"And what love do I show him in return?" So let us
ever think, and shed tears as we do so.

Communion with Christ waxes and wanes. But if
we mean to have burning hearts as believers, we need
to be persuaded that much more of heavenly joy is
possible to us than we may have thought. The purpose of the Word of God is to set before our eyes the
rich extent to which believers may be given expan-
sive enjoyments of spiritual communion with our
exalted Savior even here in this life. This is a subject
that would make the very angels sing and the stones
cry out: that God "deals familiarly with men."

We may summarize the experiences of a Christian's soul under these headings: peace, joy, love,
and hope. Each is a genuine emotion which Scripture
warrants us to feel — to feel deeply and passionately
at times.

The peace which believers have is both objective
and subjective. It is our objective ground of peace
that Christ is our propitiation (1 John 2:2). Our peace
is not the carnal "peace" of unbelievers who have
no wish to hear us speak of Christ or of the gospel;
the worldly man's peace is that of a man asleep and
so unaware of his approaching destruction. On the
contrary, our peace as believers is based on the Word
of God, which cannot lie: "He [*i.e.* Christ] is our
peace" (Eph. 2:14). Again, "Therefore being justified

by faith, we have peace with God" (Rom. 5:1). This is our objective ground of peace. But it is supplemented by an inner, or subjective, peace. This peace is in our heart and we feel it. It is spoken of in the Bible as "the peace of God, which passeth all understanding" (Phil. 4:7). None have this but such as are united by faith to the Lord Jesus, who is our righteousness.

Secondly, the joy of believers is a lively inward excitement generated by the agency of God's Holy Spirit by which we feel our hearts moved to gladness and to happiness because Christ has done all things necessary to put us right with God and to make us fit for heaven at last.

Thirdly, the love that we feel is both active and passive. No doubt all love is so. "We love him [*i.e.* Christ] because he first loved us" (1 John 4:19). The ever-blessed Son of God so loved us that He took on Him our nature and, as the God-man, He lived in this world for us, died for us, and ever lives now to make intercession for us (Heb. 7:25). To crown all His abundant love for us, this same glorious Lord is now "preparing a place" for us in His Father's "house" above (John 14:2). It is a believer's happiness to love this mighty and triumphant Lord, who is soon to come and take him to the "wedding feast" in heaven above!

Fourthly, the Christian has hope. It is referred to as a "good hope through grace" (2 Thess. 2:16). He is to "rejoice in hope of glory" (Rom. 5:2). His soul is stirred by the inward activity of God Himself: "Now the God of hope fill you with all joy and peace in believing, that ye may abound in hope, through the power of the Holy Ghost" (Rom. 15:13).

Dear reader, what heavenly happiness the Christian has through communion with Christ!

16

Our Union with Christ
in the Sacraments

The union which believers have with Christ is symbolized, or illustrated, in a host of ways in the Word of God. At the highest level, it is represented in some of the very names of God that He Himself has chosen to use: "the God of Israel," for example. This form of God's name occurs in the Bible over twenty times. It indicates that God in Christ regards Himself as peculiarly associated with His own elect people. In Old Testament times, this was with the nation or, more properly, the believing portion of the nation, of Israel, or the Jews.

In New Testament times, believers may draw near in prayer and address God with the title of "Our Father." The God who rules the universe and who counts the stars, the God who is adored by the whole heavenly host, has put into the mouth of His dear children this sweet term of address: "Our Father." God is "not ashamed to be called *our* God" (Heb. 11:16). Indeed, God is not ashamed to be referred to as the God of any individual believer who loves and serves Him. Hence, He allows Himself to be referred to as "the God of Abraham, Isaac, and Jacob."

However much some may wish to make God remote and entirely transcendent, the God of the covenant of grace is pleased to be associated intimately with those who are in spiritual union with Him. Thus God is "our God" (Rev. 5:10) and "the God of our fathers" (1 Chron. 12:17). Happy indeed are those who have had this God as their "dwelling place in all generations" (Ps. 90:1)! Happy are those who have vital fellowship with God and who can cry out, "This God is our God for ever and ever: he will be our guide even unto death" (Ps. 48:14).

Throughout history, God has chosen to have this union with His children "sealed" and symbolized by sacraments. In this visible way, it has pleased God to separate for Himself those who are in an especially close and intimate relationship to Himself. In Old Testament times, from the days of Abraham unto Moses, God appointed the sacrament of circumcision, by which every male child in this chosen family should bear in his body a visible mark or sign that he was related to God within a privileged, covenant relationship.

The symbolism inherent in circumcision is explained in Scripture. It is intended to show by a physical mark that the person concerned stands, at least by profession, in the position of one "putting off the body of the sins of the flesh" (Col. 2:11). In other words, the mark in the flesh is a sacramental sign that the person who bears it is, at least by profession, forgiven of his sins and has put the love of sin out of his life.

Sacraments are not to be understood superstitiously. People may be as much saved, blessed, and loved by God without a sacramental sign as with one. There appears to have been no sacrament from Adam to Abraham, and yet we know that there were many eminent saints in that early period. Furthermore, in the period after Abraham, no sacramental sign was given to the females within the holy family of God, but that in no way reflects on the eminence of many female believers in that period who had as firm a bond of union with Christ as male believers.

In the days of Moses, God added a second sacrament, that of the Passover. In this annual festival, the covenant people of God were required to remember their glorious deliverance from the bondage of Egypt. The main part of this sacrament consisted of their eating the flesh of a lamb, duly prepared for this special religious purpose.

The symbolism and association of ideas bound up with the Passover sacrament are intimately related to the concept of union with God. Clearly, the duty of remembering the night of the exodus from Egypt itself served to convince and confirm the minds of God's people in that age that God was uniquely *their* Savior and Deliverer. God's relationship with them had no parallel in all the other nations. They were to remember this continually and, at the Passover, they were to remember it with God-given ceremonies and symbols. The desired effect was to produce in their minds the realization that they were "a peculiar treasure unto me [i.e. God] above all people: for all the earth is mine [i.e. God's]" (Ex. 19:5). Their privilege was extremely great. This covenanted nation was to be unto God "a kingdom of priests, and an holy nation" (Ex. 19:6).

There was also in the Passover ceremony a further illustration of the union which exists between God and His chosen people. This was conveyed by the requirement to *eat* the Passover. Eating is participatory. It is a physical assimilation of what God has provided for our sustenance and nourishment. So was this sacrament of the Passover. It illustrated the great truth that the nation of Israel was in that period of history uniquely chosen to feed upon the spiritual grace and truth that God provided for them through the means of grace He instituted at that period. These means of grace consisted of the tabernacle and later temple services, and of the inspired teaching of their prophets, whom, in the course of the years, God would raise up for them. There was nothing like these things in all the earth. The nation's spiritual life was nourished by God, with whom they had a fellowship and a union in grace.

We might point to a further aspect to our perception of the sacrament of the Passover and its importance as a means of teaching God's people of old about their union with Him. It is the truth, now very clear to us, that the choice of a "lamb" by God in that period of history was itself significant. How far the pious Israelites of that age understood it we may not know. But John the Baptist made it obvious in his own ministry when he pointed to Christ, the promised Messiah, as "the Lamb of God, which taketh away the sin of the world" (John 1:29). Our spiritual food is Christ. Indeed, all who ever had any spiritual life in them from the beginning of the world have had it from only this one source: Christ, the Son of God.

God gave two sacraments, then, in Old Testament times to Israel: circumcision and the Passover. Similarly, in the New Testament age, God has given two sacraments to His church: baptism and the Lord's Supper. There is a correspondence between these. First, there is the sacrament of initiation. In Old Testament times, it was circumcision; in New Testament times, it is baptism. Secondly, God has given a sacrament of spiritual nourishment, which He requires to be taken, not once, but regularly. In Old Testament days, it was the Passover; in these last times, it is the Lord's Supper. We are not left to our own wisdom in observing a similarity in these sacraments. The Apostle Paul writes to the following effect: "In whom also ye are circumcised with the circumcision made without hands, in putting off the body of the sins of the flesh by the circumcision of Christ: buried with him in baptism, wherein also ye are risen with him through the faith of the operation of God" (Col. 2:11 – 12).

The apostle means us to understand that believers are spiritually changed by the new birth. This was so in the times before Christ and is so now. The crucial change we have had, if we are united to Jesus Christ, is what regeneration has brought about in our life. Circumcision symbolized this spiritual change then; in our day, baptism has replaced circumcision. The two sacraments both symbolize the same crucial change which those in union with the Lord Jesus Christ *must* have (John 3:3, 5, 7).

In a word, these two sacraments are illustrations of the new birth. And they are illustrations which God has chosen to give to His covenant people as a matter of obligation. The sacraments as such do not regenerate but are pictorial of the "putting off of the flesh" and the "washing away of sin" which each of these two initiatory sacraments respectively illustrates. It is extremely important in speaking of the sacraments that we do not slide into the ever-present danger of making them into converting or regenerating ordinances. They are not given, in other words, to bring about regeneration, but to illustrate it and so to "seal" it in the regenerate — at either the time when they receive the initiatory sacrament or in later life. The danger of equating circumcision with the new birth was a very real one in Old Testament times. That is why God emphasized the need for "circumcision of the *heart*" (Deut. 10:16).

Neither circumcision, therefore, nor baptism ought to be looked at as identical to regeneration.

Someone may be baptized and not be regenerated. Conversely, someone may be regenerated without baptism. For example, Nicodemus was utterly ignorant of the need for the new birth until he met Christ, though he was a deeply devout Jew. There is always need to say emphatically that, important as the sacraments are, they do not convey spiritual life automatically of themselves.

It remains to say that the Lord's Supper also points very clearly to the spiritual union and fellowship that believers in New Testament times have with their Lord and Savior. So Paul can write, "The cup of blessing which we bless, is it not the communion of the blood of Christ? The bread which we break, is it not the communion of the body of Christ? For we being many are one bread, and one body: for we are all partakers of that one bread" (1 Cor. 10:16–17). Clearly, when we take the Lord's Supper we make a profession before men and angels that we feed on Christ crucified — and yearn to do so forever.

17

The Union of Christ and His People Reflected in the Psalms

The union that believers have with Christ must not be thought of as distinctively or exclusively a New Testament doctrine. The Scriptures of the Old Testament also refer to the near relationship of the people of God to their Redeemer. The union that Christians have with God in Christ in this Christian age is not different from, but the same as, that which Old Testament believers had. As we are in Christ today, so were they in Christ equally. The church of God is one in all ages.

The main differences are these. First, in Old Testament times this privilege of fellowship with Christ was largely confined to the Jews, whereas in this age it is extended to the Gentiles also. For this reason, Paul speaks of Jewish believers as the "natural branches" and of Gentile believers as branches of a "wild olive tree" grafted in contrary to nature (Rom. 11:17, 21). That is why we who are Gentile Christians should have a special regard for the Jewish people.

They are our "elder brother," as it were, and should be held in high esteem because God was pleased to take them to Himself before He called us Gentiles.

It is true that God has largely turned away from the Jews currently. But He will one day in the future call them to Himself again. They have "stumbled" through unbelief for a time (Rom. 11:11), but God's plan one day in the future is to "graft them in again" (Rom. 11:23). And Abraham, David, and the Old Testament saints were as much in Christ as New Testament believers are today. This is a wonderful comfort. The church of God is one: "One fold, and one Shepherd," says Christ (John 10:16). We Gentile believers should pray daily that God will bring in the Jews again. They are "beloved for the fathers' [i.e. patriarchs'] sakes" (Rom. 11:28). Never suppose that the Old Testament saints belonged to God in some inferior sense compared to Christians today—all belong to God through a vital, spiritual union.

There is, more obviously, another sense in which the union of Old Testament saints might be said to have been somewhat different than it is for us today. It is in that we today, in the full light of a completed Bible, have fuller revelation given to us on the subject of our union with Christ. God's revelation in the Bible has been given progressively. What the old saints and prophets but partially saw in their day is seen more fully now in ours. Thus Peter can write, "Unto whom [i.e. the Old Testament prophets] it was revealed, that not unto themselves, but unto us they did minister the things, which are now reported unto you by them that have preached the gospel unto you..." (1 Peter 1:12). So, the union of all God's people in all ages has been with God in Christ. But we now, in the full light of the completed canon of Holy Scripture, can understand the nature of this union more perfectly.

That said, we may turn to the book of Psalms because there, in a remarkable way, God was pleased to shed light on the subject of the union which believers of all ages have with Christ the Mediator.

Let us, in opening up this fruitful theme, be persuaded that the Psalms give us very wonderful light on Christ in every aspect of His person and work. The prophetic element in them is proof that they are given by God, who alone could foresee the events in Christ's life and ministry coming to pass exactly as the prophetic Psalm-writers said. Let doubters and scoffers say what they will; they must face the fact that the prophecies of the Old Testament came to pass—and will yet come to pass.

In Psalm 2, we see the unbelieving world raging in anger against God and against Christ. God is the object of their anger. But their rebellious spirit is folly; God in heaven laughs at the rage of puny men. Here is the comfort of all believers. God's eternal "decree" is to set Christ as "king" upon the "holy hill of Zion" (Ps. 2:6–7). "Zion" is God's church on earth. The nations may and will rage against God's people, but all their menaces will come to naught. "If God be for us, who can be against us?" (Rom. 8:31).

In Psalm 22, we have an extraordinarily complete prophecy of the sacred sufferings and crucifixion of Jesus. No candid or unbiased reader could fail to be amazed at the detailed correspondence between the sufferings of Christ as given here and the description given of them in the four Gospels. This psalm is the crucifixion of Christ related a thousand years before it took place. Our holy Savior fully understood all that the psalm predicted and felt the force of its meaning to Himself as its sufferer. But, in the very heart of Psalm 22, there is reference to the union Christ has with those for whom He suffers and dies: "I will declare thy name unto my brethren," He exclaims (Ps. 22:22). Our Lord as Prophet would rise and ascend to glory, and there He would declare the gospel to all His elect people. He does this by sending out preachers to give us the gospel.

Similarly, in Psalm 40, Christ refers both to His saving work and to those whom He comes to bless. Burnt offerings, He declares, have no moral value and cannot take away the guilt of man's sin. Therefore, He affirms, He will come to do in His own person and by His sufferings what the blood of bulls and goats cannot do: "I will delight to do thy will, O my God: yea, thy law is within my heart" (Ps. 40:8). Then, says Christ, more will be needed: "I have preached righteousness in the great congregation" (Ps. 40:9). This is the means by which He summons His elect to partake of the benefits of His blood shedding and redemption—by means of preaching.

Psalm 45 refers with extraordinary sweetness to the union of believers with Christ. He is said to be "fairer than the children of men" (v. 2). However, His church also is addressed with words of exquisite tenderness and intimacy: "So shall the king greatly desire thy beauty: for he is thy Lord; and worship thou him" (v. 11). The church is "all glorious within" (v. 13) and will at last be summoned to "enter into the king's palace" (v. 15). So Christ and the church are to be together in holy love and blessed fellowship forever.

In Psalm 69, we again see Christ suffering agony and cruel rejection as men put Him on the cruel cross of shame. Christ says in the Psalm, they will give Him "vinegar to drink" (v. 21). This, as every Bible-reader well knows, was fulfilled literally and exactly (see Matt. 27:48; Mark 15:36; Luke 23:36; and John 19:29–30.) Every one of the four Gospel-writers confirms for us the inspiration of the prophecy given here in Psalm 69. Our Lord, in His deep sufferings, was offered vinegar by His cruel persecutors. But Psalm 69 shortly after goes on to address the elect for whom Christ so suffers: "The humble shall see this, and be glad: and your heart shall live that seek God" (v. 32). Christ's sufferings will bring all His elect people to glory.

In Psalm 89, we are shown how God the Father "laid help upon one that is mighty" (v. 19). The reference is to Christ, whom God has anointed (v. 20) and before whom God will "beat down" all who hate Him (v. 23). God will make this anointed Person to be His "first-born, higher than the kings of the earth" (v. 27). God's "covenant will stand fast with him" (v. 28). But then we are introduced to the "children" of this eminent Person (v. 30). Of them it is said that their sins will be "chastened" with the rod, but they themselves will not be destroyed, because Christ's "seed shall endure for ever" (v. 36). Here again, the basis of all our pardon and of all our blessings is in this great reality: the bond of spiritual union we have with the Lord Jesus Christ.

Finally (for here we take only some examples), in Psalm 110, we see Christ seated at the right hand of power and ruling over all mankind: "The Lord said unto my Lord, Sit thou at my right hand, until I make thine enemies thy footstool" (v. 1). Then we see that the reign of Christ is of two kinds. He reigns over His implacable enemies with deadly power. They are put to a fearful death: "The Lord at thy right hand shall strike through kings in the day of his wrath" (v. 5). Terrible will be the final end of all who reject Christ: "He will fill the places with the dead bodies; he shall wound the heads over many countries" (v. 6).

However, there is another aspect to our Lord's kingship. He will subdue a people to Himself in love, so that they believe in Him and readily come to Him for the salvation He has purchased for them by His sufferings: "Thy people shall be willing in the day of thy power" (v. 3). The means whereby Christ will do this is not by terror or sword, but by a mysterious, yet effectual, regeneration: "the womb of the morning." It is to be the start of a new life. It is to be a day in which the elect, hearing Christ's sweet gospel voice, will by it be made holy.

Thus, in the book of Psalms as in all the other Scriptures, we are shown this mystical union between the eternal Son of God, Jesus Christ, and those whom God has given to Him to save, renew, sanctify, and bring to glory.

No doubt such Scriptures were pointed to by our Lord Himself when He expounded to the two on the road to Emmaus "in all the Scriptures the things concerning himself" (Luke 24:27). In the light of these glorious promises and prophecies, our Lord rebukes our unbelief: "O fools, and slow of heart to believe all that the prophets have spoken: ought not Christ to have suffered these things, and to enter into his glory?" (Luke 24:25–26).

Reader, what a book the Bible is! Do you read it daily and make it your constant meditation? If you find the Bible hard to understand, pray to God to do for you what He did for His disciples two thousand years ago: "Then opened he their understanding, that they might understand the scriptures" (Luke 24:45).

18

Man's Instinctive Desire for God's Fellowship

Man was made for fellowship with God. Augustine, in his famous "Confessions," explained this instinctive sense of our need for God which all men, in spite of our sin, feel: "Thou hast made us for thyself and our heart is restless until it finds its rest in thee." The explanation for this instinct is that man is made in the "image" of God (Gen. 1:26). Although sin has ruined our relationship with God, yet we cannot escape from the strange, persistent instinct in us all to worship something outside ourselves and to give it our homage and adoration. If man does not have the true God, he will make one for himself. Only when we find God through faith in the Lord Jesus Christ can we enjoy the fellowship with the true God for which we were originally made.

The tragedy of the unconverted man is that he is inwardly at war with the only Being whose fellowship can make him fully happy and content. Man knows of God's existence, but he does not like to acknowledge or confess it. Sin has estranged him from God. We know that God exists, but we would like to hide from Him because we are aware of our unfitness to appear before Him. All the false gods and false religions on earth are proofs that man, even fallen man, is created a religious being. If we do not have God, then we must make a substitute for Him. Alas! No substitute for the true God is able to fill our heart with joy, peace, and happiness. God is the real fountain of life; all others are "broken cisterns" (Jer. 2:13).

Because God's fellowship is extremely precious, we commonly witness emotion, even great emotion, when people are first converted to faith in Christ. The heart of a sinner is overwhelmed when the pure waters of heavenly joy and peace flood into his heart. He has never felt what he now feels. To have God through faith in Christ is to have new and strange emotions. Light floods the soul. All things suddenly fall into place in the mind. The heart is filled with complex emotions of joy and sorrow. Repentance and faith mingle in the soul. Now, for the first time, we begin to love God and to be displeased with ourselves that we never loved Him before. Now, and not beforehand, we realize how desirable God is and how empty we were without Him. Now, as we never imagined previously, God becomes more important than all else in the world.

To the worldly man, all this is "foolishness" (1 Cor. 1:23). The worldly man has learned to enjoy his substitutes for God: his pastimes, amusements, trivial pursuits, and matters of tiny importance. The worldly man has taught himself to suppress all his instincts for God or for heavenly enjoyments. But he cannot fully do so. From time to time, he has painful reminders that there is a higher, unseen world to which he shuts his mind. The voice of conscience occasionally summons him out of his worldly ease to fear the awful possibility of a great God to whom he must give account. The voice of death, perhaps in his own circle of family or friends, breaks into his reverie and reminds him that he, too, must go to the grave some day. The worldly man's habit is to run away from God. His ambition is to be happy without God. He flees for refuge into atheism, agnosticism, or materialism. He has his little stock of arguments for defending his godless life to his own conscience. But, alas, he cannot know peace. "There is no peace, saith the Lord, unto the wicked" (Isa. 48:22).

The worldly life is both a delusion and a deceit. It is an attempt to live in a world that has no existence in reality. And because the souls of godless men are cut off from fellowship with their Maker, they cannot know the fullness of joy which comes to the heart of the true believing Christian. The worldly man is living in a "fool's paradise." His world of thought is false and it must crumble to nothing when he dies and faces God in the judgment. His world of little pleasures will end forever when he meets God as his Judge. Hell is the place to which all go who did not love God in this life.

How different is the experience of all those who walk with God in this life! They, too, were once "dead in trespasses and sins" (Eph. 2:1), but now they are alive to God and they experience daily fellowship with Him. To the child of God, nothing is as precious as his enjoyment of God's daily companionship. In the Bible, it is called walking with God (Gen. 5:24). There is a wealth of teaching and of meaning in that expression. This "walk with God" is full of experience along the journey of life.

The day begins with God. The humble believer rises to read a portion of God's Word in secret worship. He then prays in secret, imploring God's help, guidance, and wisdom for the day. He casts all his cares upon God. He thanks God for all His mercies. He intercedes for his family, for his church, for his nation—indeed, for the entire world. He looks at the world as God's property, the most cherished part of which is the worldwide company of believers.

Having begun the day with God in secret, he then gathers his family and he reads a portion of God's Word to them and prays for and with them before they start the duties of that day. If there are people known to be sick, in the hospital, in trouble, or dying, he prays for them and brings their needs before the great God.

Then, the man who walks with God goes forth to the duties of the day. Because he is "walking with God," he shares his thoughts, fears, and cares with God throughout the day. In a word, he talks to God as to his Father — not because he must, but because he may.

To "walk with God" is to live in good conscience with God and with men (Acts 24:16). It is to desire to do good to all whom we meet, to wish well to all, to forgive all their injuries against us and to repay all who harm us with love and kindness. The only vengeance a man seeks if he "walks with God," is the vengeance of love: "If thine enemy hunger, feed him; if he thirst, give him drink: for in so doing thou shalt heap coals of fire on his head" (Rom. 12:20).

The man who "walks with God" ends his day as he began it. He gathers his family together and with them sings God's praises, offers thanks for the mercies of the day now ended, and prays for God's protection on His people through the darkness of the night.

There are experiences of God's love to be enjoyed in this life if we are in real fellowship with God. The Bible does not hide from us the comforts and joys which gracious men and women may experience, from time to time, as they walk with God through this sad and empty world: "The Spirit itself beareth witness with our spirit, that we are the children of God" (Rom. 8:16). We refer to this as our "assurance"— the sweet, inward operation of the Holy Spirit by which believers are reassured that they are in a right relationship with God and are, indeed, regarded by God as His own dear children.

The privilege of God's children is to have experiences of heart and soul of which the world knows nothing. God puts a sense of Himself in every faculty of the soul. To have fellowship with God is to have Him in our mind as the object of continual thought and contemplation. All that we see in creation gives us some impression of His presence and power. All that is beautiful in nature reminds us that God's mind is utterly beautiful. The world in which we live, after all, is filled with created things that originated in God's mind as His thoughts. Every created being began as a thought in God's mind. To walk with God in this life, therefore, is to walk, as it were, through a panorama in which all the creatures tell us something about their great invisible Maker. How wise are His ways and how profound His thoughts! How blessed are those who have God as their friend—and how wretched are they who have God as their enemy! God is the best of friends—and the worst of enemies.

All the other faculties of a believer's soul are also affected by his union with God in life. We view God's love as so precious that we are constrained by it (2 Cor. 5:14) to live to His glory by obediently keeping to the path of His revealed will. Our memory, too, is continually exercised with thoughts of appreciation for all the goodness He has shown us throughout our life in this world. Also, our affections are roused to worship and adore Him repeatedly throughout the day as we recall our mercies from His hand. Our conscience is ever on the alert to warn us when we go astray so that we might quickly repent of each foolish word spoken or every unbecoming action.

If we are to "walk with God," we must love what He loves and hate what He hates. This is the condition of a life spent in union with Christ. "Can two walk together, except they be agreed?" (Amos 3:3). The worldly minded person forfeits heaven after death. He also forfeits the foretastes of heaven here below which true believing Christians enjoy as they strive to "put off the old man" (Col. 3:9) that they might enjoy, as far as they can in this life, unbroken communion with God. Be life's trials what they may, the man who walks with God knows that very soon he will "dwell in the house of the Lord for ever" (Ps. 23:6).

SCRIPTURE INDEX

The Inner Sanctum of Puritan Piety:

John Flavel's Doctrine of Mystical Union with Christ

J. Stephen Yuille

In *The Inner Sanctum of Puritan Piety*, J. Stephen Yuille demonstrates how the doctrine of the believer's union with Christ lies at the heart of the Puritan pursuit of godliness. He analyzes the whole corpus of Flavel's writing, showing how this mystical union is set upon the backdrop of God's covenant of redemption and established on the basis of the person and work of Jesus Christ. Chapters on the nature and acts of this union help readers gain a better understanding of what this union is, while chapters on the blessings, fruit, suffering, evidence, joy, practice, and hope associated with this union show more fully the experiential direction of Flavel's approach to theology.

Paperback, 140 pages   978-1-60178-017-1

The Law of Kindness:
Serving with Heart and Hands
Mary Beeke

"And be ye kind one to another," begins Ephesians 4:32. Christians are called to this standard, but how seriously do we take it? In *The Law of Kindness,* Mary Beeke examines the idea of kindness, shows how it is developed, and gives helpful advice for putting it into action, with specific chapters addressed to wives, husbands, parents, teachers, and children. Readers will be struck by their own lack of kindness, captivated by God's kindness toward us in Jesus Christ, and motivated to cultivate more of this precious virtue.

Paperback, 250 pages   978-1-60178-029-4

Night of Weeping

and

Morning of Joy

Horatius Bonar

Horatius Bonar, a well-known nineteenth-century minister called "the prince of Scottish hymn-writers," was also a prolific writer of scriptural, practical, and experiential Christian literature. Two of his books that bore considerable fruit and have often been reprinted were *The Night of Weeping* and *The Morning of Joy,* here reprinted under one cover. *The Night of Weeping* expounds compassionately and beautifully a biblical view of suffering, showing how it is an integral part of belonging to God's family, how to cope with it, and how it benefits the believer. The chapters on the purifying and solemnizing fruits of suffering are themselves worth the price of the book. *The Morning of Joy* shows how God leads believers to rejoice in the present and future joys of the living church, particularly through fellowshipping with the resurrected Christ. The chapters on the majestic kingdom of Christ and the superlative joys of glory are most uplifting. By the Spirit's grace, both books can be life-changing; they present us with a clear, powerful, profound, and balanced view of the Christian life and of God's dealings with His people.

Paperback, 240 pages   978-1-60178-032-4

"Trading and Thriving in Godliness": The Piety of George Swinnock

J. Stephen Yuille

George Swinnock (1627–1673) was a gifted English Puritan, known for his vivid illustrations of biblical truth. In *"Trading and Thriving in Godliness,"* J. Stephen Yuille highlights Swinnock's conviction that godliness is the primary employment of every Christian. Yuille's introductory essay analyzes the influences on, groundwork for, and expressions of piety in Swinnock's life and thought. The book's fifty selections from Swinnock's writings exemplify his teaching on the foundation, value, pursuit, nature, and means of godliness, as well as its motives.

Paperback, 235 pages   978-1-60178-041-6

Heirs with Christ:
The Puritans on Adoption
Joel R. Beeke

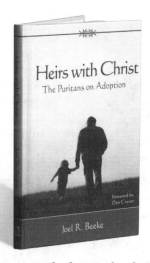

The Puritans have gotten bad press for their supposed lack of teaching on the doctrine of spiritual adoption. In *Heirs with Christ,* Joel R. Beeke dispels this caricature and shows that the Puritan era did more to advance the idea that every true Christian is God's adopted child than any other age of church history. This little book lets the Puritans speak for themselves, showing how they recognized adoption's far-reaching, transforming power and comfort for the children of God.

Hardback, 140 pages   978-1-60178-040-9

Our God
Octavius Winslow

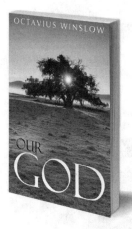

In *Our God,* Octavius Winslow (1808–1878) examines several of the perfections of God revealed to us in Scripture. Rather than advancing a comprehensive study on the attributes of God, Winslow limits his discussion to some of the moral perfections of God, such as His love, patience, comfort, and grace. With the Bible as his guide, Winslow goes beyond treating these perfections as mere abstract attributes of God. Instead, he presents the character of God as it meets the varied conditions of His people. Winslow demonstrates how the perfections of God harmonize with the particular needs of the church, most particularly in Jesus Christ.

Paperback, 164 pages

978-1-60178-005-8